Drawn to
The Living Water

Drawn to
The Living Water

Twenty Years of Spiritual Discovery

WAYNE RAPP, RICK HATEM, ANNE RAPP

SPIRITUALITY NETWORK

ASSISTING THOSE WHO THIRST FOR SPIRITUAL GROWTH

SPIRITUALITY NETWORK

ASSISTING THOSE WHO THIRST FOR SPIRITUAL GROWTH

The Spirituality Network, Inc.
444 East Broad Street
Columbus, OH 43215
(614) 228-8867 / (614) 228-8975 (fax)
Email: spiritnetwk@hotmail.com
www.spiritualitynetwork.org/

FIRST EDITION
PRINTED IN THE UNITED STATES OF AMERICA

ISBN-13: 978-0-9814530-0-2
ISBN-10: 0-9814530-0-7
Library of Congress Control Number: 2008903361

Cover photo: Liz Kaercher
Book design/illustrations: Janice Phelps Williams
www.janicephelps.com

*Dedicated to the guiding Spirit
and to Noreen Malone, OP,
who turned her contemplative thirst
for spirituality into a quest,
and to the Dominican Sisters of
St. Mary of the Springs
who supported her in that
collaborative endeavor. And also
to the dedicated women and men
who followed Noreen's vision and
gave their time, effort, and
financial support to create
the Spirituality Network and
sustain its ripples for twenty years.*

Dominican Sisters Maxine Shonk,
Noreen Malone, and Carol Ann Spencer

ACKNOWLEDGMENTS

The Spirituality Network has always been characterized by the generosity of those involved. This book could not have been written without the contributions of many people. First were those who were willing to tell their stories, relating not only their experiences with the Network, but sharing their individual spiritual quests as well.

Sister Maxine Shonk played a pivotal role in the production of this book by reviewing the drafts and providing additional detail to flesh out the Spirituality Network's twenty-year history. Her opening "Parable of the Well" set the tone for the story that followed.

Renowned poets, Edwina Gateley and Mary Oliver, generously allowed two of their works to be reprinted in this book. Holly Bardoe, a talented local poet and Wellstreams graduate, contributed several original poems to this effort.

Liz Kaercher, Dan Schleppi, and Sandra Kerka contributed their photographic talent. Liz's inspired photograph is the model for the Network's logo and the cover design of this book.

Pat Gibboney, Amanda Stone Cushing, Carol Ann Spencer, Sharon Reed, and Barbara Davis also reviewed drafts of the manuscript and were a source of inspiration and encouragement especially at a time when it looked (to the authors) as if the book would never get published. Pat, in particular, worked very hard to find sources of grants and/or other funding to meet production costs.

The Spirituality Network board continued its support of this program throughout the writing process and took a leap of faith by voting to authorize its production even when they were not sure there would be a source for funding.

Father Ralph Huntzinger, an angel with a gentle smile, stepped forward at a critical moment and provided funding for the book's production. His gift is given to honor the long-time effort of Sister Noreen Malone, the Spirituality Network's founder.

Anyone who has been around the Spirituality Network knows that Sister Noreen has been its guiding force. Such is the case with this book. It was her dream to honor the twenty-year history of the organization, and *Drawn to the Living Water* could not have been written without her inspiration and support.

CONTENTS

Parable of the Well

The Kingdom of God
is like the woman
who comes to the well
with the thirst of a weary traveler.
The dust of the journey
weighs upon her soul.

As she approaches this place of refreshment,
she sees again, as if for the first time,
her reflection there on the surface,
returning her gaze with questions
she has not asked before
and recognitions
she has not yet allowed.

As if to reach beyond the reflection,
to break through the image,
to plumb the depths of its questions,
she casts her bucket into the well.

The bucket
sinks deep into the water,
far beneath the place of the familiar reflection.
The deeper it plunges,
the darker the waters become
until the bucket is surrounded by a darkness
that is total and complete
and where it gathers
water that is clean and sweet.

In the fullness of time and grace,
she brings it to the surface,
struggling
with the weight of realization.
It takes a long time
to pull the bucket up from the depths.
It requires patience and courage.

But when at last
she has completed her task,
she rejoices,
for hers is the purest of water
and the sweetest of refreshment.

She shares it joyfully with her family
and with all those who are thirsty saying,
"Look how I have been blessed!"
And blessed she is, as are we
Each time she approaches the water of life
To plumb the depths that await her.

So is the Kingdom of Heaven for all those
    who seek God
and who can let go into the depths
with patience and courage.

~Maxine Shonk, OP

FOREWORD

I stand in awe and gratitude for the last two decades as I ponder the path the Spirituality Network has followed and the place it has had in the spiritual journey of so many. The story of the Spirituality Network is one that is continually evolving. So the word "history" does not do justice to the purpose of this book. *Drawn to the Living Water* represents a reverent and grateful pause to look back and to notice how graciously God has led us thus far in this evolution; to acknowledge the gift we've been given in the Spirituality Network, and to trust that the Divine Process that brought us here will continue to take us where we need to be in order to address the spiritual thirsts of our world.

The Spirituality Network came to be not because of a particular vision of a final product or in response to a mandate from any church authority. It did not even come as an imagined solution to a perceived problem. It was not developed from a business plan or from a blueprint for success. The Spirituality Network came to be from a simple awareness of great poverty — a poverty of spirit — my own and that of so many around me. And I heard a familiar refrain, "*Blessed* are the poor in spirit for theirs is the kingdom of God."

Through my encounters with thousands of people in both rural and metropolitan communities, through countless retreats and faith sharing sessions and one-on-one companionship, I discovered in so many the same spiritual thirst that I had identified in myself. It was a thirst for the God of Life, for the God who breaks into the "everyday-ness" of life and shows us the "something more" we are called to be.

I would frequently ask, "When have you experienced God most powerfully in your life?" The answers often came in the context of the birth of a child, or the death of a loved one or falling in love . . . always in the midst of questions, or suffering or pain and always in the context of the daily encounters with life. The stories of God's breakthroughs were endless, and all of them left the storyteller with a burning thirst for more − an inner thirst for a deeper relationship with God.

I knew that thirst, too. I discovered it in myself when I and my congregation of Dominican Sisters struggled for renewal in the wake of Vatican II, when life as we knew it was drastically changed by the challenge to reclaim the spirit of our founders and to embrace the radical message of the gospel. I remember being challenged by the words of my Dominican Sister, Margie Tuite, whose work for peace and justice in the 60s was tireless. She assured me that the surest path to renewal was to "stay close to the poor" the poor within and the poor without. I discovered that my relationship with God was deeply connected to a reverence and acceptance of the giftedness and need in myself and all those others who were naming their thirst as well.

I knew the answers to the questions that arose in this thirst lay deep within each person, where "God dwells in our innermost being" (Ps. 139). I saw and heard this thirst in the people I met along the way. We were all drawn by our thirst for the God of Life (Ps. 42), invited to come to the waters of baptism and to drink. The Spirituality Network grew out of that movement of the Spirit in all of us. In its twenty years, it has lived faithfully into its name, nurturing and empowering the "Spirituality" of all God's people in central Ohio wherever we find them, regardless of faith traditions and building a blessed "Network" of connection and community.

The Spirituality Network was built on a solid Dominican foundation, initiated by a proposal written by a few Dominican sisters at the congregation's 1986 chapter. As such, it has consistently embraced and held sacred founding principles that distinguish it from most business models in the nonprofit world.

First and foremost its "CEO" is the God who called it into being and who opens our eyes to the spiritual needs around us. Meetings are conducted in a spirit of prayer and discernment. It is Spirit driven and need based. There is no power structure or business plan that dictates its direction but the Spirit that moves within each of us and is shared freely among us.

It is collaborative, ecumenical, and mutual in its programming and in its deliberations. The gifts of many other organizations and individuals are acknowledged and pooled, thus creating an environment that both empowers and entrusts the spiritual journey.

There is an itinerancy about the Network that frees it to go wherever the needs of the people call it. Hundreds of parish missions, retreats, and spirituality programs have taken us to some of the remotest parts of the state of Ohio — places of worship, places of education and of social change. It has set us down among the homeless, the imprisoned, and the outcast.

It is my hope that the readers of these pages will see themselves as more than observers or listeners to a story. May they see themselves as part of the mission of the Spirituality Network, as conduits of its story, as bearers of its message of hope and light, and as the next best movement in its evolution.

–Noreen Malone, OP

PROLOGUE

I *had finally talked myself into going,* but now, driving slowly down the street looking for the address, I wondered if I would really follow through with the scheduled meeting. I spotted the house number and drove past it, deciding, instead, to leave my car on the other side of the small park across the street. The short walk might give me time to get my thoughts together.

I wasn't sure why I'd let myself get talked into meeting a stranger to talk about my spiritual life. Several days earlier, I had broached the subject with a woman I'd known for years. We went to the same church, and she'd always struck me as someone who had it together, who openly lived her faith. Linda wasn't an overly pious woman, what some people would call a "goody-goody." She was down-to-earth and real, and she was one of the most caring people I'd ever known. I admired her, and when we'd run into each other downtown and were sharing time over cups of coffee — just two women enjoying each other's company — I opened up to her and revealed what I thought of as my flagging spiritual life. I remember telling her that I felt like I was going through the motions most days. She didn't lecture or try to fix me. Instead, she started telling me about some of her own feelings and how she was involved in something called spiritual direction that helped keep her focused on developing an ever deepening relationship with her loving Creator. She had my attention, and, as she continued to talk, I found myself wanting to be in that same place. When we parted that afternoon, she gave me the name of her spiritual director and suggested I get in touch with her. That's how I came to call Jean and accept her invitation to learn more about the process.

Now, walking across the park, I was hesitant. I wasn't the type who shared my feelings easily, even with people I knew. How would I be able to have an honest conversation about something so personal as spiritual growth? And yet, I knew that it was something I yearned for. I wanted to have it, to be on the other side of the process, not sure I had the smarts, the strength, or the stick-to-it-iveness to reach that goal.

Halfway through the park, a scene unfolded to the side of me. There was a small basketball court enclosed in a chain-link fence. Standing at the gate outside the fence was a small boy. Being too short to reach the latch on the gate, he was trying to get the attention of a large man playing basketball by himself. The man was wearing earphones, shooting and rebounding the ball, seemingly unaware of the boy's calls. I continued walking but never took my eyes off that scene. It was my own spiritual plight that was playing out. I was outside the fence trying to get in, while an unconcerned God was involved with his own pleasure and ignoring me.

I knew then that I would go through with this meeting. I wanted to find a way for God to pay attention to me. I wanted to talk to God. I wanted to have God invite me inside the fence to play.

When the door to the house opened, the smile that greeted me was full of love and acceptance and gave me hope that I had come to the right place. Jean took me in, made me feel at home immediately, and over tea, she began asking about my family. I could see why Linda liked her; they seemed so much alike to me — two open and friendly women. And I felt, even though I had shared nothing yet about my spiritual life, that I was in the presence of an accepting woman as well.

"You know," Jean said, "when Linda called me and asked me to talk to you about spiritual direction, I quickly knew what I would say. There is one word that best describes the process: JOURNEY. Spiritual direction is a journey, a wonderful journey of exploration that helps move you toward a more meaningful encounter with your creator, the source of all love and understanding."

I was taking in what she was saying, nodding to her as if I understood.

"I think one way I can expose you to the process — if you're interested — is to make a comparison to something that's very important to me." She moved across the room and returned with a large loose-leaf binder and placed it on the coffee table between us. "I'm involved with an organization called the Spirituality Network, and I have been from its beginning. We're celebrating our twentieth anniversary, and we've put together our history." She patted the binder tenderly, as if it were a holy book. "It's all here in this book, the voices telling the stories. Organizations, like people, must follow a spiritual journey in their development. If you're interested in understanding journey, it's right here. I'd like to tell you how and why this journey began, and if you're still interested in knowing the whole story, I want you to take the binder when you leave today and continue to follow the journey. After you've read the story of the Spirituality Network, we'll talk again, and you can tell me if you're interested in pursuing your own journey." She offered me a warm smile. "Whether you know it or not, you've already started."

Jean put on a pair of glasses, opened the binder, and began to read.

The Sharing

We told our stories —
That's all.
We sat and listened
To each other
And heard the journeys
Of each soul.
We sat in silence,
Entering each one's pain
And sharing each one's joy.
We heard love's longing
And the lonely reachings-out
For love and affirmation.
We heard of dreams
Shattered
And visions fled.
Of hopes and laughter
Turned stale and dark.
We felt the pain
Of isolation
And the bitterness
Of death.

But in each brave
And lonely story
God's gentle life
Broke through
And we heard music
In the darkness
And smelled flowers
In the void.
We felt the budding
Of creation
In the searchings

Of each soul,
And discerned the beauty
Of God's hand
In the muddy, twisted path.

And God's voice sang
In each story.
God's life sprang
From each death.

Our sharing became
One story
Of a simple lonely search
For life and hope
And oneness
In a world which sobs
For love.

And we knew
That in our sharing
God's voice
With mighty breath
Was saying
Love each other
And take each other's hand.
For you are one
Though many
And in each of you
I live.
So listen to my story
And share my pain
And death.
Oh, listen to my story
And rise and live
With me.

~Edwina Gateley

DRAWN TO THE WATER

Sister Noreen Malone, a Dominican Sister from St. Mary of the Springs community in Columbus, Ohio, first noticed what she called "the thirst" in the late 1970s. After twenty years of teaching, she had accepted a new calling. She traveled the twenty-three counties of the Catholic Diocese of Columbus as representative of the Vocations Office and eventually as Vicar for Religious.

"For me personally it was the ten years of working in and traveling around these twenty-three counties that I noticed the thirst," Noreen says. "I couldn't name it right away, but it was there. People would ask about it in very different ways." The people Noreen encountered wanted to know if there was a place where they could find support, where they could feel safe, a place to believe and trust, where they wouldn't feel that they were on the fringe of acceptance. In visits with priests, ministers, and religious, many shared with Noreen that they had few resources to guide people in prayer and spirituality. As she recognized the thirst in others, Noreen knew that it resided within her as well. "There was a deep knowing within me that regardless of gender, race, culture, religion, orientation, nationality — whatever our differences — we all have a thirst for the Holy One, the Divine. This thirst draws us into relationships with one another and propels us to people we would never think of approaching."

Noreen's thirst drove her to seek spiritual direction, to make directed retreats, and attend spiritual conferences, sharing her reflections and listening to others do the same. As Noreen continued to travel and listen to people express their deep inner thirst, she realized that she was being called to address their needs in some way. But how? A dream began to form, one that would require her to take a new direction in her life and follow a new calling.

After leaving the Vicar's role, Noreen studied spirituality at the Shalem Institute in Washington, DC. The prevailing practice at Shalem was the presence of God's Spirit guiding every aspect of life in every moment. "All I had to do was notice," Noreen says. "Finally I felt like someone understood my unquenchable thirst. I realized that nothing I could do on my own would ever satisfy the deep yearning within me, and that this persistent thirst was God's way of drawing me into a contemplative relationship with the God of Life." Gradually Noreen became aware that her thirst was common to all human hearts, and it was the seed from which the Spirituality Network grew.

Jean finished reading and closed the binder.
"That was the beginning," she said to me. "One woman recognizing the same thirst in herself that was being expressed by others. A woman with a dream that knew she was being called by the Spirit to do something that would give life to the dream. There wasn't a name yet. Just a thought. But you'll see that if you continue reading."

She offered the book to me with a smile. I took it. "Thirst" was the word I would have used to describe my own spiritual condition. I was interested in this story. I did want to see how a single thought can grow to something grand and good. Jean didn't give me a time frame to return the book, just said I knew where to find her when I was finished reading it.

When I trudged across the park toward my car, I glanced at the basketball court. It was empty.

That evening after dinner, instead of watching another rerun of a show that wasn't particularly good to begin with, I opened the book and began to read on my own.

A PLACE OF SPRINGS

Ellen Dunn is also a member of the St. Mary of the Springs Dominican community. She is a pastor and preacher at Holy Family Church in Beech Bottom, West Virginia. In 1985, she had just moved back to Columbus from Boston where she had been studying. "I remember the dream to offer spirituality opportunities to people in Central Ohio," she says, "and we wanted to have a program to train lay people for spiritual direction. We did not know how to get there, but it really was something we deeply wanted, and we started to look at who we had to work with and what background they had, their credentials and how we could utilize them."

In 1986, Noreen, Ellen, Carol Ann Spencer, and several others proposed to their Dominican congregation that their community might research the ways that St. Mary of the Springs, the only motherhouse of sisters in Central Ohio, might address the spiritual thirst in the wider community. The Dominican leadership began to explore ways of collaborating in an effort to establish a Spiritual Life Center.

"The leadership, God love them," Noreen says, "didn't know what to do, except try to study it." Six months later, the leadership asked her to chair a committee.

"I was given the freedom to choose anybody I wanted to be on this committee. It really was a freedom given to me that I think was of the Spirit. The leadership did not feel a need to oversee it in any way. When I think about this, I really marvel that they allowed the Spirit the freedom that was needed at that time."

Noreen did not want a committee that would just study the life out of the dream. She wanted dreamers on her committee, those who could envision something different. She knew the group had to look at spirituality in ways that were different from the normal approaches of institutional churches.

Among Noreen's group of dreamers were five Dominican sisters from St. Mary of the Springs, a married couple, and a Dominican priest. This group shared basic guiding principles and a deep understanding that the endeavor would not be a business or a church, nor was it a replacement for church membership, but rather a different model of ministering together. So from this place of Springs a vision was conceived. Three pillars held up the vision from the outset: to supplement what the churches are able to do; to be itinerant, going out rather than have people come in; and to offer spiritual direction and retreats for those for whom such spirituality opportunities were otherwise unavailable.

Noreen explains the need to be itinerant. "The ten years that I worked in the diocese I traveled the twenty-three counties over and over again. People resented that everything happened in Columbus when they lived in Portsmouth or they lived in Dover. So built into the Network was this expectation that we would have teams of people who would be willing to go where the folks were."

Thus began the Spirituality Network — thirsty people seeking the only One who can satisfy. The question then became: how do you represent the organization visually?

Liz Kaercher is an associate member of St. Mary of the Springs Dominican congregation. Liz described the coming to be of the Spirituality Network logo this way: "I had known Sr. Noreen for a few years when, sometime in the early 1980s, she told me of a dream, a hope that she and others had for the formation of an nondenominational group of laity, clergy and religious who would reach out to others to address the thirst for the God of Life. Knowing that this is a common thirst or hunger for each of us, my heart responded to this dream with excitement. I wanted to be part of this endeavor.

"A few weeks before one of the committee meetings, I went away for a long weekend to a lake for a private retreat. I am a camera buff, so I took my camera with me. Sitting by an inlet off the lake, with a small island across the way, I was throwing chunks of stale bread into the water for the ducks and watching the rings of water flow outward for some distance from the center. I was meditating on God's love for us and how this same love is meant to spread outward from ourselves, and beyond ourselves, to embrace others. I took a few snapshots. Later, when the film was developed, I was pleased with one of the photos especially. The outward rings were prominent as was the deep reflection of the trees and the sun in the water."

Liz took the photo to the committee meeting. Noreen liked the photo, and after sharing it with others, asked if Liz would allow it to be used as the visual for the Spirituality Network logo. Liz's responded with a resounding "Yes!"

This was the perfect image for one who can let go into the depths. For having done so, one cannot help but overflow into the wider world.

Of the logo photo, Noreen says, "Many people are truly thirsting for the God of life and are being drawn into the depths of the inner journey of faith. But the journey inward always will compel us out again, urging all of us to be preachers of the Word until the ripples of Good News have brought the reign of God to all the world. We are most grateful to Liz Kaercher for the logo picture."

I closed the book and looked at the photo on the cover. I hadn't paid much attention to it before, but now, knowing its history and what it represented, I looked at it with new eyes. It was a marvelous representation of the effect the Spirituality Network wanted to have on a thirsty population. I lay the book down on the table and picked up the phone. I wasn't ready to quit reading yet, but I knew I couldn't go on before I talked to my friend, Linda, who had gotten me involved with this idea of spiritual direction. I had a question that needed answering.

I had not talked to Linda since she suggested that I contact Jean, so I had to bring her up to date. She was thrilled that I was exploring the history of the Spirituality Network.

"I have a question for you," I said. "I've enjoyed reading about Noreen and the other sisters that got your program started, but I'm just curious about your involvement with this organization. It's so Catholic and we're both Protestant. I still remember when I was a kid that we didn't go to their church, and they weren't allowed to come to ours."

Linda laughed. "I haven't changed religion if that's what you're asking. I don't secretly go to Catholic Mass on Sunday before I come to our service. That's what's so great about what's happened through the Spirituality Network. It's nondenominational, and we simply build on our common beliefs, learn from each other, and offer our time and talents to bring the quenching waters of our faith to others who are thirsting for it."

"I hope you don't think I'm turned off or deliberately being negative" I said. I just wanted to know how people with my faith and beliefs fit into the picture."

"You've gotten ahead of yourself," my friend said. "If you're really concerned about the question of a place for your faith, you can look ahead in the notebook and find the chapter that talks about the ecumenical foundation of the Network. If you'll let the story reveal itself, though, you'll find that the Protestant contribution to the development and continuation of the Spirituality Network is very strong and well represented."

When I hung up the phone, I did thumb forward in the book and saw that there was a chapter on ecumenism. That satisfied me, so I returned to my place in the story and started reading the next chapter.

LOOKING AT THE REFLECTION

I n the early days, as the Spirituality Network began to evolve, it became important to name its mission. The founders knew that they would be an organization that would reach out and provide opportunities for people to encounter themselves in a journey toward deepening spirituality. Reach out, yes, but to whom? Provide opportunities to encounter one's spirituality, but with what resources? There was tremendous potential that was both a blessing and a challenge. A blessing in that there were many needs the spirituality ministry hoped to meet. The challenge was to develop a focus with boundaries that would define the emerging Spirituality Network as it strived to respond to the great thirst.

Prayerful monthly meetings led to a steering committee that committed to the gradual evolution of a spirituality ministry with qualified persons already involved in this type of work. A budget was developed to support committee work and also for the ministry expenses of one full-time person. The initial budget covered setting up an office at the Dominican Motherhouse. The office took requests, and networked with spirituality ministers for offering prayer, support, visioning, planning, and involvement. The center began inviting and empowering new persons to develop their gifts for ministry and initiated collaboration with other Catholic religious congregations and orders serving in the Columbus Diocese.

In an effort to glean what people saw reflected back to them at the well, Noreen surveyed the religious congregations and communities, soliciting ideas on how individuals and religious communities might be able to contribute in collaborative efforts. Responses were diverse. Some wanted to reach persons who may not otherwise be ministered to, such as the handicapped, aging, and poor. There were those who wanted to collaborate in spiritual direction for ongoing spiritual growth. Retreat work and a resource group for spiritual growth for married couples were other named desires. Many wanted to be part of a dynamic that affirms gift-edness and empowers one another to give and receive. With the Spirit as leader, the idea of using the gifts of all to help people claim their dignity and birthright to the Kingdom was expressed. Others wanted to offer growth opportunities for all who were interested in their spiritual life. There was a desire to establish a center for individual and small group retreats where caring for the earth, offering hospitality, sharing excess, living simply, working toward change in systems – not as a large institution, but a small site capable of enabling many other diverse groups and individuals to augment the work. One expressed the hope, that with a variety of trained people – lay and religious – the Network would minister especially to those in pain spiritually and to those who seek spiritual nourishment.

Rather than focusing the work of the Network, all of these responses served only to reflect again how widespread the thirst was. The best that could be gleaned was that the mission of the Spirituality Network would be simply to attempt to meet the needs for spiritual growth wherever they were found. (Coincidentally, this was part of the mission of the Dominican Order worldwide.) The Network would establish a broad approach to meeting the needs of those seeking spiritual growth and be welcoming companions to those who came.

Cindy Kuhn was one of those people. She worked many years in a medical laboratory and then, for a brief time, as an admitting rep in a hospital. After that, Cindy studied Clinical Pastoral Education and worked as a chaplain. Cindy eventually left hospital chaplaincy and has been making jewelry ever since. She says, "I love my life. I've been a hermit for probably the last two years. A recluse is what I usually call myself. I literally dropped out of everything. I mean *everything*. I just felt I needed to be totally alone.

"I don't know what 'spiritual' means," Cindy says. Then she adds, "Except that I have to tell you that the Spirituality Network came into my life at a time when I was asking questions that nobody else had answers to. It was a group of people who were nutty in the way I was nutty. It wasn't the Network, per se, that drew me, but these lovely people. They were awesome people — people who were kind and interesting."

Cindy goes on to express a belief that can be threatening or liberating. "They were spiritual in a way that wasn't religious. That felt good to me. I didn't feel like I was the thorn on a rose bush as I did in some of the other groups I was in. At the Network I began to be invited into these places where there was this supportive, encouraging environment for somebody who was seeking answers to 'Where is God in the midst of all this?' And understanding the question — that was the beauty of it. I didn't have to explain what I meant.

"One of my callings was to demonstrate how art was a part of my spiritual journey, how art helped me come to understand what was going on in my life. I knew it had meaning, but I didn't know how or why. It wasn't the Network, per se; it was when I was working on a master's degree in theology in Dayton. I took a course on Jungian perspectives of spiritual direction and thought, 'Oh my God, that's what I'm doing; there's a name for this.' The more I explored the underpinnings of my own journey, and what this art was doing inside of me as it was coming out, the more I became excited to share that experience with other people. It was one of those things that you don't know you know until somebody else reinforces that you know it."

Cindy pauses and becomes more reflective as she continues. "I told somebody, I feel like I'm on this boat, adrift. And God is absolutely trusting that wherever I drift to is perfectly OK. However far I go, it's OK. Scott Ropin has a wonderful song about it. He says, 'Bring you home to stay. When you've gone down every road. and every map is worn and torn, I will bring you back home.' I'm thinking that's God's philosophy. In my world, God keeps going after the sheep that escape the gate."

Loretta Farmer also came to the Spirituality Network. She is a member of Our Lady of Perpetual Help Catholic Church in Grove City, a Columbus suburb. She says, "I remember years ago thinking, 'All I have to do is have a good job, a house, and two nice cars, and I'll be fine.' Once I had all that, I wanted more. I was thirsting for more. I had always been the type of person who went to church and was involved in some type of church community. What happened in being involved with Noreen and the Network was that for the first time in my life, I found a place that would nurture my personal experience and relationship and recognition of God. Not only in church but in individuals and in situations, and not only wonderful, joyful situations, but hard, messy, situations. That was a whole new opening for me, and it made all the difference in my life."

Noreen says, "I think that's probably the principal part of spirituality that's different from our religious experience, to remind people over and over again that it's in the messiness; it's in the messiness that God speaks to us."

Loretta adds, "I think, as I have moved through the ministry and have become a spiritual director, it is like this whole new awareness that everyone is involved, and it's not just for the ordained or religious, or whoever is involved in the leadership. It is also for the ordinary folk like me. That was a whole new revelation for me. I think that's what I see the Network continuing to do, inviting people to that place, that safe place where they can talk out loud and say anything — they won't have to worry about being judged — and let them grapple with stuff, rather than needing to provide people with answers."

Loretta has explored various ways to live out her faith. Like Cindy, she also studied Clinical Pastoral Education. Additionally, she worked as a hospital chaplain, and she says, "There was still something missing." Looking back over her life, Loretta realizes, "It all fits together. It's the whole journey. At Shalem, I was so aware that I could not have completed that experience without everything that went before. It's all part of integration. We don't have to tear out the weeds yet. We can leave them in there. That was very powerful for me to know that I didn't have to get perfect. What happened to me is I moved from trying to get perfect, go to church, etc, in order to be OK with God to knowing I was already OK. And not perfect. For the first two years that I was in spiritual direction, Noreen would ask, 'Loretta, do you believe that God loves you just the way you are right now?' Every time she said it I would burst out crying, because I didn't believe it. It was such an important piece, and that is what the Network has taught me: It's OK to be messy; it's OK to have struggles. You don't have to get perfect to belong to the flock. It's kind of like we went back to the original purpose of religion: for the sinners.

"And no matter how hard it is, once you get that taste, you can never go back in the box. I know I can't. I'll die in there. I would rather move forward and meet the opposition than stay back and die on the vine. I know that in my heart, even though it's hard. And I think more and more people are discovering that. It's incredible. God is alive and well. There are a lot of people who are really thirsting. And when you see that realization of God's living water on someone's face, it's like watching a birth. That's what the Network has done for me and other people. I found a place where I can live and breathe."

As I sat the book down, there were tears in my eyes. I thought of Cindy drifting, and God saying, "That's OK." She knows that wherever she goes, God will always bring her home. And like Loretta, I was a person who needed to be affirmed, who needed to know that I didn't always have to get it right as long as I kept trying.

I knew what Loretta meant about "dying on the vine." That's the way I felt. She had found and recognized God in the hard and messy places of her life. Why couldn't I? I lay my head back in my chair and closed my eyes. I felt so alone, and that made me angry at myself, because I wasn't alone. I had raised three children who were an important part of my life, and I had a husband who I knew loved me. Why couldn't I see my family as blessings? Why did I feel so lonely? I had a home and financial stability and things many people didn't have, and yet I felt empty and deprived.

Some times when I looked at my husband, I wondered what drove him, what pleased him. He was good-natured and accepting. Too much so, I thought. He sat back and took life as it came, while I wanted to grab hold of it and shake it and get something else out of it before I died. I didn't want this to be all. I wanted so desperately to have life be more than this. For me to be more than I was. And, most of all, I realized, Noreen's question haunted me. Did I believe God loved me the way I was right then? With all my doubts and feelings of emptiness? I knew the answer was no.

I sat the book aside and prayed for God to show me what I needed to do to gain the acceptance and joy I read into Cindy's and Loretta's stories.

Oh God!
Help me to let go of all the things
I think I need and/or worry about.
Grant me the grace to listen
To the silence where You speak
To my heart.
Let me embrace all that I am
And praise You
For the gift of my life.

RIPPLING OUT

He summoned the Twelve and began
to send them out two by two ...
Mark 6:6

O ne of the Spirituality Network's first efforts in community outreach centered on parish missions and retreats. Noreen says of this effort, "Some of us were part of teams for parish missions, where in the course of three or four days of conferences and communal prayer, we would offer to meet with people. And those appointments, oh my goodness, I have goose bumps just as I think about it. They were people who were looking primarily for spiritual direction, but they didn't have a name for it. That's how we began to get people who were interested in it, and just the thrill of seeing their faces when we would invite them to that, or explain that to them, like, 'Who me?' "

Marilyn Larkin is a Catholic and a member of Our Lady of Perpetual Help in Grove City. Marilyn has been associated with the Network since its beginnings. She explains that, for her, the real growth came in shared prayer, wonderful hospitality that pervaded the setting and the opportunity to do outreach work.

Marilyn went with Jeanne Purcell and Barbara Goodridge, a Franciscan sister, each week to Faith

Mission and later to the shelter on Broad St. in Columbus to meet with homeless women. "The Network provided refreshments for the body, and we fed and were fed by the spirits of the women we met," Marilyn explains. "That experience was a great blessing for me and led to my involvement in the start up of a group for women at St. John's Episcopal Church on Town Street. The support group is called HER PLACE."

Marilyn and three other women went there with Noreen. "We still meet twice a month," she adds. "Pastor Lee Anne Reat and the women there continue to inspire me."

The Network provided an opportunity for outreach for Cindy Kuhn as well. Cindy recalls being asked, "'How about you getting involved in this?' or, 'How would you like to be involved in this retreat?' or this, that, or the other thing. So, it wasn't like navel gazing or something like that." Cindy remembers a retreat where women from Upper Arlington (an affluent Columbus suburb) and women from the inner city came together. She says, "We did this retreat that was centered on the theme of basket weaving and how our lives are inter-connected. There are certain givens we come in with, and there are certain things that we bring to our life. The women made baskets that were all different, so it illustrated the point. It was just really a marvelous, exhausting time. I don't even know how I ever had the energy. It was so important, and I was so filled with passion about it. My passion just drove me deeper and deeper."

Commitment to the poor was a strong component of the Spirituality Network from the outset. Approximately half of the people receiving spiritual direction were not able to offer a donation when the Network began. Grants from the St. Mary of the Springs Justice Fund and the Notre Dame Justice Fund made it possible for Noreen and Pat Pieper, a Sister of Notre Dame de Namur, to travel to Portsmouth in southern Ohio monthly for group spirituality with poor women.

Pat says, "That for me was just the most — I don't know — truthful experience I guess of understanding how things just happen. It's funny, I think one of the things that happens in the Network is people learn from people without even knowing that you're learning something. I remember the women in Portsmouth were so scared in the beginning, as we probably were because we didn't know what we were doing either. The kind of letting down barriers when they began to talk to each other, that was the most exciting thing. We had some little lunch prepared or somebody brought it in. But when they started helping each other and talking to each other. 'Oh, you live here,' and they had lived in the same complex without knowing each other for who knows how long. And all of a sudden they began helping each other. Saying, 'I can do this or this.' It's just amazing all the people who have been touched: that's the nature of the Network."

Pat says that she didn't remember much about the Network's organizational part, but she did recall Noreen's trust in the process. "We would make our lesson plans on the way down to Portsmouth. We would have some little thing, some poem or something. And then as it happened and as it grew, it did so much for me in terms of being myself and knowing I could facilitate this thing. It was more believing this can happen when people come together. We can just talk and somehow be freed. It was freeing for me just to be able to do it, and then to see it happening with the women. Then I left in 1990 to go to Arizona. My involvement was really short; but I know for me it had a lasting effect. When I went to Arizona, I had a degree in counseling and was working in a sexual assault counseling agency, which didn't really work out. But I met a wonderful woman who was a certified counselor. We decided we would work as a team with women adult survivors of sexual assault. I saw it happening on a different level in a different form. Women came together and were free to talk about their lives. A few months after my return to Ohio, I got a letter from a woman and she said, 'You taught me so much about letting it happen.' "

The St. Mary of the Springs Dominican congregation supported this evolving model of ministry with a limited budget, office space, personnel and transportation. By November 1991, the Spirituality Network had evolved to the point of providing spirituality ministry in many places and in many forms. Noreen had some health problems that year and wrote to the resource members to thank them for the support and prayers during an illness that had lasted several weeks. "I feel very blessed to be surrounded by such loving, prayerful care. I'm slowly coming back to health and am very aware of the need to 'pace' my schedule a bit more. I count on your continued understanding in the months to come."

That Noreen was able to pace herself a bit was due in part to having a new partner at the Spirituality Network. Maxine Shonk, also a member of the Dominican congregation at St. Mary of the Springs, joined the Network staff during the summer of 1991.

"Maxine," Noreen said at the time, "has certainly been a Godsend these past three months. I'm afraid that my sickness has been the occasion of Maxine's 'baptism by fire' but she has more than proven equal to the demands."

The Spirituality Network now offered a Directed Prayer Weekend Series, evenings of reflection for Ministers of Care. The Network also offered a semiannual Interfaith Weekend for those living with HIV/AIDS and their caregivers on the theme: "Healing Our Images of God." An ecumenical team of clergy, religious, and health professionals, along with persons living with HIV, facilitated the retreats. The Network regularly provided spiritual direction and prayer/support groups.

The outreach program of the Spirituality Network was also touching the women of Holy Rosary/St. John on a weekly basis. The meetings created opportunities for women to share their stories in a safe space.

Noreen remembers that they were drawing women from the Homeless Foundation and Friends of the Homeless. "This Women's Awareness Program has become a very important part of our ministry and a very valuable experience for us personally," she says.

Through all of these early endeavors of ministry, it was easy to see the appropriateness of the visual that the Spirituality Network had chosen for its logo: the outward ripple effect emanating from the depths of the inner journey of faith, radiating the Good News to all the individuals and organizations that it touched.

TROUBLED WATERS

For the first ten years, the Network was subsidized by the Dominican congregation of St. Mary of the Springs. Noreen and the early supporters knew that this arrangement could not continue forever, and they set a goal to become financially autonomous by 1994 and formed an Advisory Board to help figure out how best to achieve it.

The board consisted of people with various gifts and expertise, and Noreen gave them the benefit of her thinking on the matter. "I feel caught in the tension between the dream and the reality," she told them. "We cannot continue to network for nothing and expect to assume responsibility for our own finances. All financial experts tell us no endeavor can survive relying on grants alone. We need your input and your prayer in what has become our primary concern at this point in time."

The Network hoped to be self-supporting and consulted with financial experts on methods to achieve that status. There were legal concerns as well. Legal consultants addressed the concerns regarding spirituality ministry, especially that of spiritual direction.

Lori Buonauro, one of the original Advisory Board members, reviewed the Network's financial picture over its four-and-a-half year history, establishing a figure of $72,000 per year as the minimum required to be self-sustaining. Lori explained that grants were difficult to obtain, since few grantors support administrative costs and even fewer programs support spirituality. Because the Network saw itself as ecumenical, it could not be included in the Kennedy Directory, which listed only Catholic organizations approved by their local bishop.

Geoff Albrecht, also a board member, suggested the first move toward autonomy might be incorporation as a not-for-profit organization. Incorporation would release the Catholic Diocese and the St. Mary of the Springs Dominican congregation from liability and reduce confusion regarding the Network's independent status. Incorporation would also identify the Network as an independent entity, and grantors might be more open to contribute. The not-for-profit standing would also provide a tax-exempt status. After much discussion the Network Advisory Board believed incorporation was a good option.

The immediate goals of the Advisory Board, other than becoming financially self-sustaining, were creation of a training program for spiritual directors and obtaining facilities to house the Network. They knew that they would have to depend on the St. Mary of the Springs Dominican congregation in the near term to achieve these goals, and they needed help from the congregation and its leadership in researching educational programs for training spiritual directors.

The Network also wanted to create a collaborative model reaching beyond its Dominican and Catholic roots to other denominations, religious congregations and agencies in order to provide more comprehensive service to the people of God. The Network's diverse offerings led to Advisory Board questions on who and what the Spirituality Network was, and how it would evolve in the future. Identity questions were present since the early days. In truth, identity and financial questions would continue to be constant themes through the years. With an Advisory Board in place and a plan of action, the Spirituality Network looked forward to the next decade. What would the Spirituality Network be in another ten years? The Advisory Board expressed hope that in February 2002, the Network would continue to be all it ever was in 1992, along with being financially secure.

It was evident that the people involved in the Spirituality Network had much to be proud of. They had grown a lot in a short time and had overcome many obstacles. I didn't know any of these women, but I began to develop a kinship with them. In my mind, I could see the smiles of satisfaction on their faces as they thought about how far they'd come. But I knew, in reality, there was also concern, because their position was so tenuous and fragile.

I wanted to keep reading, but the stack of dishes that needed washing was calling to me. I pulled a pot — still caked with chili — from the stove and brought it to the sink. As I began to wash dishes, I said a prayer for all those who had worked so hard to keep the ripple of spirituality moving outward toward those who needed it. I had begun to realize that I wanted the ripple to continue.

WILD GEESE

You do not have to be good.
You do not have to walk on your knees
for a hundred miles through the desert
        repenting.
You only have to let the soft animal of
        your body love what it loves.
Tell me about despair, yours, and I will
        tell you mine.
Meanwhile the world goes on.
Meanwhile the sun and the clear pebbles
        of the rain
are moving across the landscapes,
over the prairies and the deep trees,
the mountains and the rivers.
Meanwhile the wild geese, high in the
        clean blue air,
are heading home again.
Whoever you are, no matter how lonely,
the world offers itself to your imagina-
        tion,
calls to you like the wild geese, harsh
        and exciting—
over and over announcing your place
in the family of things.

- Mary Oliver

HELPING HANDS

As the Spirituality Network continued to grow, there was a corresponding need for someone to perform as a full-time office manager, but financial limitations would not support that need. For the immediate future, the organization would have to depend on a corps of volunteers. JoAnn Meeks was an answered prayer, becoming a five days a week volunteer in 1992. Noreen said, "We are truly blessed to have her and delighted that she is willing to share her gifts in such a generous way."

Over the years several people helped with office tasks. Ann Sullivan, Marianne Reihl, and Sister Matilda Vaitekaitis put order into the Network library. Francis Gabriel Mahoney, a retired Dominican sister, was a faithful and effective volunteer. Kathy Poulton and Theresa Schneider helped with composition, typing, computing, and organizing at the Network. "The gentle spirit of each of these women helped to create a more contemplative space at the Network," Noreen said.

Another volunteer was Mary Ann Kerscher. "I didn't know what I was doing. I had never done any type of secretarial work. I mostly licked stamps and stuffed envelopes and tried to get all that out." Like all of the dedicated volunteers, Mary Ann did whatever needed doing during the times she was there, including helping to facilitate programs.

And, like other volunteers, Mary Ann felt she received more than she gave. "The Network gave me an outlet and encouragement to know my gifts and to hone them and be confident enough to use them. The Network seemed to give me a place and people to nurture my personal spirituality without bounds of the church, religion, and the almost physical boundaries that I grew up with. It opened me up to spirituality as opposed to religion. I just bloomed. I knew it was a good thing, and I knew I wanted to help it as much as I could in trying to explain to people what it was. I think a lot of people saw the same thing."

There was something else that drew Mary Ann to the Network. "One of the attractions for me, too, was the awe I had of being in a holy place. When a group of people came together it wasn't rote prayer. It was like, 'Where's the prayer?' The answer was, 'It comes from within.' That was wholly different for me coming from a Catholic background because growing up everything was rote. It was very refreshing."

The movement from rote prayer to more sponta-neous prayer was significant for many people. Cindy Kuhn was one of them. "Prior to being involved with the Network I didn't know it was OK to bless my own chil-dren. Protestants could spontaneously pray, but no, Catholics prayed the Rosary and the Our Father. It wasn't that long ago that that's how we all thought. I mean, for a layperson to lead a group in prayer that was not rote was unthinkable. Was that only twenty years ago? Now, if there's a parish retreat or a parish council meeting, it's happening, and it's accepted as self-evident. But, way back then, if there was a blessing and the priest was anywhere in sight, 'Father, lead us in prayer.' " Cindy adds. "I remember it was like the freedom to not just connect with God, but being a witness to your own relationship. It was incredibly liberating."

As much as the commitment of the volunteers was a blessing to the Network, the constant turnover could be difficult in terms of continuity. Jane Belanger is a member of the St. Mary of the Springs Dominican community and a volunteer. She assesses the contributions of the volunteers this way, "There were all those different ones who passed through. It's not so much that it didn't work, but it was like people got what they needed or gave what they had to give and then moved on. I think the history of people has been part of the history of the Network all through. It's OK. They come for a while because, whatever circumstances they are in, this works for them. Those short-term things have all done something. In some cases it brought out different skills or showed up different needs or weaknesses or lacks, and we were able to say, 'Hey we need to do something about this area.' "

Mary Ann says, "That's what I found a frustrating element, because it's unlike a business where someone is hired and will stay for a period of time for some consistency. But the sincerity of people who came onboard was very strong. Then someone would come and they would have a great idea, but they just wanted to give you that idea and then step back out the door. And those that had been there for a period of time would look at each other and take a big, deep breath and ask, 'Do we try to do this?' Because most ideas were very good ideas, if we had the people, and the place and the money. We might have one or the other, but we didn't have all of them."

Jane adds, "In some ways we thought that some people just came and left. It was always out of honesty. They thought it just didn't work anymore for them or whatever. I think the Network has really been honest; I think even to the point of hardship to itself. While those kinds of things are difficult, I think they have a pruning quality about them, too. I think the honesty thing has always been a part of any group that I have been in at the Network. The prayer and sharing that always was characteristic of any meeting or group contained a level of honesty and relational transparency that is rare."

Mary Ann sees another aspect. "The flip side of that is for the Network to honor those individuals who have discerned that it's not their time anymore to be with the group. I have had difficulty in a couple of different instances where I had to say that it was not my time anymore. As difficult as it was I knew that there was a trust that I had thought this through. So it works both ways."

If coming and going was a pattern for some of the volunteers, that was not the case for Corrine Hughes. She started as a volunteer at the Spiritual Network in 1994, and has faithfully returned to do whatever has been asked of her ever since. "It has been a graced adventure," she says. "If I could go down the alphabet and list what is stimulating about serving the Network, there could certainly be one or more values for each letter. The letter that is prime for me personally, however, is "P" — people, prayer, presence, et al. The people who gather in support of the Spirituality Network embrace these values and could add others to complete the alphabet. Like myself, they are seekers of the sacred, and they willingly share experiences and insights. My spiritual horizons have broadened being in relationship with these prayerful people. Prayer precedes and permeates all the plans and preparation for the Network projects and is an integral part of every event."

Maxine Shonk feels that volunteers brought their much needed skills and talents to the Network as well as a beautiful sense of what is sacred and holy. Corrine is a perfect example.

It wasn't just the volunteers who gave time to the Network to perform all the tasks that were needed to survive. Groups outside the organization generously provided resources that would have quickly exhausted the Network's limited finances. As a perfect example, Noreen cites Sr. Angela Marie Emerick and others at Mt. Carmel Center for Human Empowerment for handling some Network printing. The Spirituality Network couldn't have survived those early years without this type of generous support.

ATTACHING A STURDY LINE

he January 1992 *Advisory Board* *re*commendation that the Spirituality Network incorporate as a not-for-profit was acted on. Geoff Albrecht, a former student of Noreen's, used his legal expertise to develop the incorporation bylaws. Incorporation gave the Network tax-exempt status and this encouraged donations. The Network hoped its new status would help in grant applications, too. Incorporation meant the Network needed a Board of Trustees – the Coordinating Council, as it came to be known. The original Board of Trustees members were Ron Atwood, Lori Buonauro, Ellen Dunn, Barb Goodridge, Vincent McKiernan (Vice Pres.), Ginny O'Keefe, Sharon Reed (Secretary), Larry Reichley (Treasurer), Carol Ann Spencer (President) and Dick Wood. Virginia Bruen, Noreen Malone and Maxine Shonk were ex officio members. Members of this original Board of Trustees had all served on the Advisory Board that preceded it. The board (Coordinating Council) held its first meeting Sept. 9, 1992, with a primary challenge to find additional space for the growing Network.

The council reviewed a Code of Regulations for the Spirituality Network at their first meeting. Developing the code was a difficult task, as the Network wanted to comply with legal requirements and be faithful to its dream of collaborative structures. The Code of Regulations established an ex officio liaison with the St. Mary of the Springs leadership team for continuity and to help in a transition to autonomy. Virginia Bruen filled the role. The Coordinating Council was enthusiastic and eager to act for the Network. An early action established three committees: finance/development, public relations/marketing, and formation/education to address the priorities identified in January.

MORE STRONG HANDS

Dick Wood, a member of First Community Church in Grandview, a Columbus suburb, was invited to be a member of the Network's Advisory Board and the Coordinating Council that followed. Besides bringing exceptional organizational skills to the Network, Dick provided the opportunity to reach out to the Protestant community and create a more ecumenical group of spiritual seekers. Of his invitation to become an active member of the Network, Dick says, "Being a Protestant, that was really exciting for me. I had been through Shalem and had wonderful experiences there. And one of my great fond memories was being really filled with the Spirit and finally leaving the business world. Having worked at Maryhaven (a substance abuse treatment center in Columbus, Ohio), I felt like I was really ready for a spiritual life. I was called by Noreen, who said, 'Dick would you like to take off your spiritual director's hat and put your businessman's hat back on for about three years and help organize this Network?' That's one of my fondest memories."

Kerry Reed, senior pastor at Gender Road Christian Church, Canal Winchester, was an early member of the

Board of Directors. Kerry points out that Eric Weinberg joining the board was another example of the Network reaching out to create a much broader spiritual community; Eric is Jewish. Kerry says he appreciated gaining a perspective through Eric's participation on how decisions were made within the Jewish congregation. "It was such a breath of fresh air to have people outside the traditions that I understand, to speak of common things that we also often felt. We get blocked into our own way of doing things, so it helps to hear somebody else speak from another perspective. It allows a breeze to float through and maybe change an attitude." He adds, "Also, as a Protestant, it has meant a great deal to me to not just be tolerated as in 'we need a token so-and-so' — but it's never been that way in my experience with the Network. It has been 'share with us your experience, your perspective, your vocabulary, because we realize that the vocabulary we use is going to limit the participation by certain groups.' That's so true but often not acknowledged. We kind of roll along, 'Aren't we really doing well,' and 'Isn't this wonderful,' without saying there are certain words that are immediately going to turn off certain segments of our populations."

Sharry Hoch and her husband, Ron, come from different faith traditions. She admits that it hasn't always been easy over the past thirty years for the two of them to actively participate in both their Lutheran and Catholic parishes. "Prejudices and divisions still exist among our Christian churches," she says. "However, we've always felt affirmed and encouraged by Network people. They embrace ALL persons, regardless of race or religious beliefs. The fact that their programs are led by people of various religious persuasions has been uplifting and nourishing for us. One of the ways the Network has empowered me is through its emphasis on ecumenism."

That the Spirituality Network has helped many people deepen their relationship with God and grow in being true to their authentic self has helped some remain within a church or faith tradition.

Barb Davis from First Community Church is one of those people. She was attending theological seminary when she first encountered the Network. Barb says, "I've found a home and have been recognized as hungry for God." Somewhere in her process Barb remembers being told, "You need to discover God on your own and be authentic." These words helped her remain within a church while being very angry about much of church history. Her experience of authenticity put her on a path to follow one of her passions, quilting. Barb has exhibited her own quilts, co-authored a book on quilting, and leads a ministry called "Squares and Prayers" at First Community. A cluster of women gather weekly and sew, offer prayers and then present the fruits of their sewing and praying — lovely lap quilts — to folks with a wide variety of needs or to mark celebrations.

Susan Hendrickson is also a member of First Community. She is a poet and has been involved with the Network for many years. She says, "I think that's the beauty of the Spirituality Network; it has always felt truly ecumenical to me. Whatever piece I was working on or interested in exploring was accepted without any kind of bias. Just an openness to where God was taking us in this discussion."

For those of the Catholic faith whose numbers dominated the early Spirituality Network, the benefits of a truly ecumenical community have been equally rewarding.

Janice Bachman, a member of the St. Mary of the Springs Dominican congregation, reflects on the Network's ecumenical experience. "Really, when you look back on how those relationships were viewed as obstacles at that time – and I don't want to minimize it, they certainly were – but look at what grew. How much more than we might have even dreamed, actually incarnated something that was truly ecumenical."

Jane Belanger was at an ecumenical retreat center in Minnesota when the Spirituality Network began. After Jane returned from Minnesota, she, with two other Springs Dominicans, Camilla Smith and Loretta Forquer, founded Shepherd's Corner to help people recognize the importance of stewardship in nature and the environment.

Reflecting on the Spirituality Network, Jane says, "I think coming from an ecumenical retreat center it was like a breath of fresh air to find a group of people where that reality was still happening. For me, it was a way to stay connected with the broader communion of spiritual stuff."

Mary Ann Kerscher says, "I had gone through twelve years of Catholic school. Both sets of parents and everybody in my family was a Catholic. It was a time where there were nuns and priests in the grade schools who told the students 'there were Catholics in the world and there were non-Catholics in the world.' That's where I was coming from."

Marriage Encounter was her first connection to people of other denominations about spiritual matters. "And I thought, 'I'm still alive, and I haven't been struck down, and there are some really good ideas. I may have to look at this.' The people that came through — people you knew about that came through for talks and things, or just the people you would meet because of an inner city gathering — were as much a force of spirituality as this well known person. It really gave me a lot more exposure to things like that. I probably needed that, too."

Despite the fact the Spirituality Network had spread beyond its Roman Catholic roots to a more broad-based community of journeyers, there were still relatively few people who knew of this wonderful resource. The Coordinating Council asked organizations that shared their goals to endorse the Network. Initially the Network received endorsement of its work from eight organizations. The endorser groups were named on the Network letterhead so that if an individual or group didn't know the Network but did know an endorser, the credibility of the endorser could carry over to the Network. The Coordinating Council was successful in acquiring twenty-two endorsements.

ENDORSERS TO
THE SPIRITUALITY NETWORK

Adrian Dominican Sisters, Adrian, MI
St. Alban's Episcopal Church, Bexley, OH
Amethyst Inc.
St. Ann's Hospital
Ascension Lutheran Church
Boulevard Presbyterian Church
Broad Street Presbyterian Church
Sisters of Charity of Nazareth, KY
The Community Kitchen
Sisters of Divine Providence, Allison Park, PA
Leadership Team, Dominican Sisters,
     St. Mary of the Springs
Elizabeth Blackwell Center at Riverside
     Hospital
First Community Church
Sisters of St. Francis, Oldenberg, IN
Leadership Team, Sisters of St. Francis of
     Penance and Christian Charity,
     Stella Niagara, NY
Leadership Conference of Women Religious
     in Ohio and Michigan
St. Marks Episcopal Church, Upper Arlington,
     OH
Mount Carmel Health, Mission Services
     Division and Center
  for Human Empowerment
Ohio Institute of Pastoral Care
Society of the Precious Blood, Cincinnati
     Province
Peace Works, Lexington, OH
St. Thomas More Newman Center, OSU

Dick Wood says, "I think the endorsers helped spread the Network, just by the very act of going around and telling our story to different churches and groups."

Noreen adds, "We are very excited about the many public endorsements the Spirituality Network has received. The endorsers represent a lot of work and a great deal of support and encouragement of the ministry of spirituality. It is testimony to the treasure we have in our resource community. WE ARE SO PROUD!!"

With the sense of pride and elation, there was also a major disappointment. Though the Network's goals fit well with the Diocese's pastoral planning project, *Called by Faith / Committed to the Future,* the Catholic Diocese of Columbus did not endorse the Network. Diocesan administration was concerned about liability issues, particularly in the area of spiritual direction, and did not allow Catholic parishes or the diocesan newspaper, *The Catholic Times,* to publicize Network events. This decision reinforced the Network's move toward ecumenism.

Well, now I understood how the Spirituality Network had moved from its Roman Catholic beginnings to become an ecumenical organization. I found it interesting and somehow satisfying. From everything I had read so far, I felt like it would have been a shame if the Catholics had tried to make this exciting journey by themselves. And that would have gone against the inspiration they had for their logo: the rippling effect that stretched beyond what the eye could see. The sending forth of their wonderful journey of discovery.

I'd read about the Protestant churches coming onboard with their ministers and congregations. And, even in one case, a Jewish man. And why not? I firmly believed we all worshiped the same God. Why not worship together?

In this past chapter, I was also pleased to read about some of the men who were bringing their talents to the Spirituality Network. I'd seen a name or two in previous chapters, but here were stories with more detail about men joining with the women to help build the Network. They weren't trying to take it over and run it by their own rules, but they were truly signing on as partners to help build God's kingdom. This is something that I wanted for my own husband: a partner on the journey. And why should I give up that dream? I decided to turn it over to God, because I had always believed that with God all things were possible.

You created us to be free to be
And inspired the holy words that
    religions use
To remind us of our divine nature —
Each one a part of the whole of creation.
The amazing truth is that You
Empowered us with an inner authority
To respond in our unique ways
To your unconditional and lasting love.
As we journey and dream together
Give us the grace to listen to your voice
    and each other.
May we allow You to dream and be alive
    in us
And love who and what needs to be
    loved in our midst.
Help us listen, Lord. Keep us in touch —
Imagining new beginnings with a
Deeper awareness of Your presence in
    everything.
Keep us dreaming and wake us up!

PLUMBING THE DEPTHS

Just as the apostles in the early Church wrote letters to communicate with their growing and far-flung believers, Noreen and Maxine also wrote them to communicate with Network resource members. Such was the case in March 1993, when they identified a continuing problem that was quickly reaching the critical stage.

"We need to tell you that the major concern that has occupied a great deal of our time and energy is the financial need of the Network," the letter said in part. "The Dominican congregation of St. Mary of the Springs has underwritten the greatest part of our operating expenses for the last six years. After 1993 this funding will not be available due to the escalating financial demands of the congregation's aging membership. We are faced with the very real possibility that the Spirituality Network will cease to exist in 1994. We must generate a solid financial base from which to operate if we are to continue." The message could not have been more clear.

Dick Wood reflects on the importance of the finan-cial commitment of the Dominicans to the early life of the Network. "A thing that always stays in my mind is the generosity of the sisters," he says. "We couldn't have crossed the street without their generosity."

Resource members were invited to a meeting to share their thoughts on the Network's critical financial need. Noreen and Maxine concluded their communication this way: "It is frightening to think of the possibility of closure, but it is encouraging to know that we have you to help us dream and respond creatively to this challenge. Our plans for this meeting include prayer and faith sharing as a community drawn close by our God, and to discuss ways to raise funds and stabilize income. It is very important to us that we hear from you."

During these ongoing struggles, Noreen's mantra became an echo of the early Church's account of the apostles being challenged. She would often quote Gamaliel, a rabbi, Pharisee, and member of the Sanhedrin: "If this movement of theirs is of human origin, it will break up of its own accord; but if it does in fact come from God, you will not be able to destroy them . . . " (Acts 5:39) Noreen would need to repeat this quotation often to strengthen her own faith as well as that of the Network members.

After meeting with the resource members, the Coordinating Council planned the next steps to address the critical financial situation. They met with St. Mary of the Springs Dominican leadership team. The Coordinating Council thanked the Dominicans for their investment in the Network and reviewed efforts to reach financial independence. The Council hoped sharing about the Network's successes and hopes would lead the Dominican congregation to respond favorably to a request for two more years support. Their prayers were answered. The Dominican Leadership enthusiastically commended the breadth and depth of the Network's ministry. Virginia Bruen wrote on behalf of the Dominican leadership team, informing the Network that they agreed to unanimous in-kind support until June 1996.

With this financial commitment, a more diverse and professional board, and a successful collaboration with members of the faculty at the Methodist Theological School (METHESCO) on a workshop for spiritual directors from several denominations, the Network seemed to be moving forward again.

Noreen wrote another letter to Network members: "Spring brings growth and life and hope to what appears to be a withered world. Sometimes it takes spring to renew us in our hope for a brighter world by giving us a new perspective on what has always been there. This is not unlike our own personal journey as we travel through life's seasons."

She described the work of the Spirituality Network saying, "Many people in central Ohio from all walks of life, social, and economic status are gaining new perspectives on their lives through the ministry of the Spirituality Network. For some people, it has not occurred to them that their life could be any more than it is. Some simply have no access to opportunities for such spiritual nurturing. Still others feel no need to get in touch with the spiritual until faced with a life-changing event or awakening to a void in their lives. Spirituality is a universal struggle for wholeness and it is the journey we all take regardless of religious affiliation."

Noreen continued, "The Spirituality Network is a unique interfaith organization of men and women — lay, religious and ordained — trained and gifted in spirituality, scripture, and related pastoral concerns such as grief, stress, prayer, community formation, individual spiritual direction, and self-esteem. At the Network, we believe that all people should have opportunities to explore their spiritual yearnings. We are especially attentive to the poor and marginalized to whom these opportunities are less available. We are about awakening people to what is already there, about being companions on the journey and about discovering and celebrating new life and hope among us."

Noreen invited the faithful to share the Network's vision and to help "in this important and unique ministry." She asked for financial assistance and encouraged people to support the Spirituality Network on an annual, semi-annual or monthly basis.

Another approach to improving the Network's financial condition was taken by the executive committee in March 1994. Believing that the Network had two missions, spiritual development and community service, the executive committee recommended that in the short-term all Network resources focus on community service. A new description of programs and services offered under this mission was attached to the recommendation. The proposal said, "When we feel secure with this mission, and have adequate human and financial resources, we will turn our attention to Spiritual Development."

No sooner had I decided to turn the idea of my husband becoming a companion on my spiritual journey over to God, than I was presented with a ray of hope. It was one of those rare times that my husband and I were alone for dinner when out of the blue, he brought the subject up. "What's so interesting in that manual you're reading, Joyce?" he asked.

I thought his choice of the word, 'manual' to describe the book about the history of the Spirituality Network an interesting one. It was a big clunky-looking binder, but it wasn't a 'how to' book. Yet if a reader followed along, she could get a strong idea about how things worked in that organization and how the combination of the parts produced a cohesive whole. I answered simply and truthfully, "It's the history of this organization called the Spirituality Network."

"What's that all about? Why is it something you want to know about?"

I wondered how much I'd learned about the organization. I plowed ahead. "It's really about a journey, the journey we all make when we're trying to find out more about ourselves and our relation to the God who loves us."

"Isn't that what Pastor Norton does every Sunday?"

"Yes, and he does a good job of it, but I'm at the point where I need more."

"Our church has all those programs," he reminded me. "We just finished that whole series for Lent."

"And it was great, Matt. I don't know about you, but for me, something's missing. You know, there are other churches and other religions. People all over are searching for better ways to live their lives closer to the way God wants us to. The book tells how some people came together to try to learn how to do that. It just tells how things got started and where they're going. I haven't read it all, so right now I'm just exploring. Trying to find my way on the journey."

"Well, good luck," he offered and began clearing the dinner dishes.

FILLING THE BUCKET

Programs were the lifeblood of the Spirituality Network. Not only did they generate income, but they exposed many people to the organization. Spiritual direction, parish missions and other programs requested by churches and different religious organizations were conducted by a pool of over sixty resource persons all with specific and varying gifts to give. In this number were spiritual directors, massage therapists, artists, dancers, sign language interpreters, drug and alcohol counselors, computer wizards, graphic designers, writers, preachers, teachers, missions or retreats depending on their venues. Jane Belanger recalls that one of these prayerful events was a series of retreats at the Catholic Parish in Amsterdam, Ohio, that met all of the Network's objectives. Amsterdam is an Appalachian community in the eastern Ohio coal mining area, close to Steubenville. "It's going to the ends of the earth," Jane says. "The roads to get there go up and up. The pastor wanted some people coming in to preach during Lent at Sunday Mass. Individual people would go on a weekend; they preached on Saturday night and again on Sunday."

They also taught in a school program after Sunday Mass. Jane continues, "It was an effort to give the people something different. I appreciated the pastor's desire that something be different because he was the only show in town."

Noreen emphasizes the importance of the Network's contribution to the Amsterdam Parish. "I guess I was so aware of the burnout among the clergy who, in a sense, were taught to be Lone Rangers. They need to know how to collaborate. That was kind of a catchword for us too; we had to learn how to collaborate. When we were thinking of being itinerant, we were thinking of teams going out. But I think God kind of turned it around and said, 'You will all be itinerant. I will keep moving you around.' "

Among the most life-changing Network efforts were weekly gatherings with economically disadvantaged women in inner city Columbus. These were similar to gatherings that had been held previously in Portsmouth, Ohio, beginning in 1988. Women-to-Women was not a program that operated as counselor to client, teacher to student or successful to unsuccessful. It was simply women-to-women. It was a listening ministry centered on issues of empowerment, self-esteem, and discovery of one's own spirit and personal relationship with God. Participants create a safe place to simply talk, to listen to others' experiences, wisdom, and discoveries, and to reveal their own wisdom so all who gather leave with much more than they brought and recognize that they brought to others more than they realized.

Jeanne Purcell was introduced to the Network while doing volunteer work with another organization where a

Women-to-Women group met. "I am like a child of the Network; they gave birth to me. I am one among many. I was volunteering for the Homeless Families Foundation watching children while the Network conducted a group for the mothers. When the Spirituality Network moved that program, they invited me to continue participating in the same way, and I went."

A new Women-to-Women group was started at Holy Rosary / St. John in 1990. Jeanne says, "I babysat the children while the mothers were in their sessions. I remember my whole process with the Network was so incredible. I come from a background that is a wreck, a train wreck. Deeply wounded, I did not have the capacity to function at a normal level. All I had the capacity to do, really, was take care of children. People from the Network would invite me gently to participate in the groups, and I couldn't do that. I was so wounded; all I could do was be with children. I remember it was so remarkable because those children all came from the same wrecked backgrounds. And it was like the children were translucent; it was like I could see through them. Because I had that experience. I could see where they were coming from. I could understand, and it was a miracle. I think that was where the healing began."

When she thinks further about it, Jeanne says healing actually began with the unconditional love that was extended to her simply as a child of God. Little by little, Jeanne began to participate more fully. "I hung in there with the Spirituality Network, and each program I attended and each day I showed up, they showed me their unconditional love. Everybody accepted me, where I was and for who I was. I didn't *need* to be any different, and that *allowed* me to be different, and that allowed me to grow. It was such a cathartic experience."

The Women-to-Women group at Holy Rosary concluded, and Barb Goodridge, a member of the Franciscan Sisters of Stella Niagara, expanded the weekly Women-to-Women program at Faith Mission. Jeanne says Barb had an important role in her life. "Barb always made me feel like it's OK to be imperfect. She invited me to participate at another homeless shelter where she began meeting women. I actually have a background of homelessness, drug abuse, and everything else. God was working with me. I started out the first week or two, again, babysitting the children, and through the gentle love and the invitation that was always extended to me to grow, I joined the group. That was the beginning of me in ministry. Whatever that was – walking with people in that position, people who were marginalized and destitute and wounded. Somebody important said, 'Where your greatest woundedness is, there is your greatest giftedness.' That is exactly true because all the doo-doo that went on in my life before became the fertile field for what was to grow from that, which was my capacity to be able to minister and relate to these people in a prayerful way."

The Columbus meetings led to a contract for two series in women's spirituality and a twelve-step program of spirituality with Amethyst, Inc., one of the Network's endorsers, and a transitional, therapeutic facility for women recovering from addiction.

Maxine says the Women-to-Women program touched one hundred to one hundred fifty women during the first six years. "It was not a clinical group but one of support and empowerment by and for women. Its success was attributable not to any therapeutic approach – though many facilitators were qualified counselors –

but to the women's presence to one another and the safe environment in which to tell their stories and thus grow in self awareness."

She recalls a woman who was a consistent weekly participant in the program: "It was a genuine pleasure to watch her process of self-discovery and to grow in self-esteem as a result of her participation. What was once a suspicious, controlling, sometimes violent life stance has — through her willingness to search for her inner truth — been transformed into a commitment to nonviolence, compassion and continued self-discovery. The positive changes in this woman are evident in her loving commitment to her children and in self determination as she pursues further education at Columbus State."

The empowered woman became a co-facilitator for the group. Maxine remembers that the woman willingly offered the wisdom of her own experience in a way that no clinical techniques can. Meanwhile she continued to grow and to receive the ongoing support of the group — support that was unavailable to her in family or neighborhood.

The women encouraged one another to seek individual help when needed. Maxine says, "I sincerely believe that these women receive immeasurable benefit from the group, as the group does from each one of the women."

Maxine recalls an experience from another program that was a gathering of inner city women with women from an affluent Columbus suburb. "I remember one meeting with Barb Goodridge leading the session. Barb held up two flowers, a healthy crisp rose and another one that had seen its day. She asked them which one they were. And this one woman immediately chose the rose that was wilted. Without skipping a beat, she said, 'That's the one that needs God the most.' "

Noreen said this woman had leadership gifts. "We began to nurture her to facilitate. She had that gift; it was very obvious to us.

I think one of the things I remember most was that race was not a problem. We were at Holy Rosary (the inner city parish) for six years."

Today, there is a network of Women-to-Women groups, and there is a desire for more, Noreen talks about a group that meets at the Martin de Porres facility at St. Mary of the Springs. "It's been so wonderful for our older sisters to have those women come. What I hear my sisters – my community members – say is similar to the awareness that I learned in my early years: that the women who come are definitely the teachers. The sisters know that. For me that's kind of going full circle. Some of them would not have that opportunity other than for the women to be able to come there. The sisters are developing relationships with them; the women have something to teach the sisters, retired teachers. That is such a comfort to me. And I'm hoping they'll be able to expand that. That need is all over."

The weekly gatherings led to major transformations for the women who came to offer assistance, too. Curiosity got Karen Herrmann involved. She first met Noreen and Maxine on a directed retreat in the late 80s. "It was just after that time that I verbalized my interest in becoming active in the community," Karen says, "but I didn't know how or where. Maxine told me that there was a women's group held each week to assist women on limited income to identify their own spiritual path. I think I surprised Maxine when I showed up to help. At this time there was a limited number of women involved — Joanne Meeks and Jeanne Purcell along with Maxine, Noreen, and myself. We commuted these women to St. John's Church, offered them lunch and child care, and provided the space so that they could have some time to be with themselves. We slowly grew in numbers as others joined to assist with this experience. I was blessed to work with these center city women for the next three years and was greatly gifted by them. This experience most likely led me further on my own path — as these things always do — to pursue a degree in counseling."

Sharry Hoch adds, "I have been especially touched by my participation in the Women-to-Women ministry. Noreen — along with Maxine and the Women-to-Women group — gave me the courage to embrace my feminine spirituality while continuing to stay in the struggle of ministering within the church I love."

Dick Wood recognizes similar benefits in the program for women battling addiction that he created at Maryhaven. "When I was doing that work at Maryhaven, people would say, 'What a marvelous thing you've done. You're so amazing giving all that time to a horrible group of women, all prostitutes and all drug addicted.' The truth of the matter is I was learning so much about who I am every day from those women. I realized how important that is. We don't talk about it enough and it is hard to articulate. I can remember sitting there the second or third day after some of the sharing that went on and thinking, "Isn't it interesting? The son's been to prison once again; the mountains are still standing, and that woman is still OK. In spite of all the things she said her friends are still there. What is this about getting all this stuff out, and realizing it's OK to do that?' That's how subtle these things start. So, if she could do that, then maybe I could too, a little bit, just a tiny bit. That's how it begins."

Dick reflects for a moment then adds, "The two greatest learning experiences I had in my life were from women. One was at Maryhaven, and the other was being part of the Network, knowing Noreen and Maxine, and the Dominican sisters. It's significant, and it has become significant in the work that I've done in the church."

Ellen Fox adds to the program's narrative. She was looking for a spiritual director when she met Noreen during a retreat. Ellen says, "Noreen's greatest gifts to me were really hearing my story and then her witness that she believed that God was alive and acting in my life. Noreen helped me discern my call to massage therapy, and as soon as I had my license, she blessed my hands in the most sacramental moment I have experienced. She then invited me to participate with the Network."

Ellen has participated with the Network in many ways, including working on retreats and as a board member. "I began working on holistic and HIV retreats. The holistic retreats were good, and two stand out particularly. The first was a joint retreat with women from Holy Rosary/St. John (a Columbus center-city parish) and women from Arlington (an affluent suburb), a powerful combination. The next was a group of home- less women. We on the team laughed all night at our presumptuous thinking that we had anything to give to these amazing women."

Ellen also participated in interfaith retreats for those living with the HIV virus. "The HIV retreats were invita- tions into the lives and deaths of some amazing people.

I was forever changed by the way our paths touched. For me, the HIV retreats hold the fondest memories and have been the most life changing."

Dominican sister, Germaine Conroy, initiated and planned the first retreat with the assistance of Damien Ministries in Washington, DC. The Network collaborated with the AIDS Service Connection, the Mission Services of Mount Carmel Health and the Dominican Sisters in presenting the bi-annual, four-day interfaith retreats with men and women living with the HIV/AIDS virus. The retreats emphasized healing images of God, self, and the world.

Jay Jackson, a member of the Spirituality Network retreat team, experienced first hand the impact of those days of giving and sharing. "Many people with HIV and AIDS in the early years of the pandemic were ostracized by their faith communities and had no spiritual connection to help them cope with the disease," he says. "A common response was self condemnation, a sense of hopelessness in life and toward death, and it was to this situation that the Network hoped to bring a healing ministry of presence and acceptance."

The weekends were structured so as to ease participants into sharing their stories more deeply and to be able to hear acceptance and affirmation from the facilitators and other participants. Jay remembers that a beautiful part of the weekend was the memorial service on Saturday evenings. "It was often the first chance participants had to remember lost loved ones in such a setting," he says. "But it was also bittersweet, because many of those early participants knew they themselves would be memorialized in some subsequent service."

During these retreats, participants came to experience the blessing of love without judgment and to realize their own ability to be a blessing to those around them in deeply spiritual ways. With the closing of the AIDS Service Connection, it seemed that the retreats had run their natural course and had served the purpose that the Network believed the Spirit had in leading the organization to develop this ministry.

The Network has offered many and varied retreat days and weekends for those involved in the ministry of care. One series of holistic retreats was offered for nurses in the Mount Carmel Health System in Columbus, Ohio. The series began when Colleen Gallagher, OP, Vice President of Mission for Mount Carmel, contacted Noreen to discuss the special needs and concerns of those who work with the sick and dying. Often those who minister to others in the sacred journey of life can face emptiness or burnout unless they are renewed and their spirits replenished. The theme of these retreats was "Care for the Caregivers" and was also available to those who are home caregivers for spouses or loved ones.

In 1993, the Spirituality Network became the official sponsor for the presentation of a series of Community Building Workshops made available through the Foundation for Community Encouragement in Ridgefield, Connecticut. M. Scott Peck, well known as the author of several books, including *The Road Less Traveled*, was the developer of the workshops. In partnership with First Community Church and under the able leadership of Dick Wood and Sandi McCall, both specifically trained in facilitation by Peck, the workshops were held semi-annually for three and a half years. In this unique program design, community happens as much in the silences as in the words and was in complete sync with the Network's vision of living out of a contemplative space.

While the preparation and presentation of programs were often time consuming and difficult, there were moments of levity that were pure joy. Maxine recalls working with Noreen to develop a program on one such occasion, "We were doing this mother-daughter retreat on the sixth floor of the (Dominican) motherhouse, and, of course, we had to make the meal, and set the setting, and do the environment and all. Just the two of us. And we must have had thirty people coming for this mother-daughter evening. We were making the salad for the meal and planning the retreat at the same time. We were going to do a midrash and I thought, 'We've got to find women in the Bible,' and what we came up with was Moses and how his mother and his sister were responsible for saving his neck. I remember very much the reaction to it; we just got into the roles. Noreen was Mama Moses, and I was Miriam."

Maxine triggers Noreen's memory of the event. "I remember on the sixth floor we had all these huge plants. We moved all the plants and had the Nile River. We had to find bulrushes somewhere and a basket. Every time Maxine did not know what else to say, she would look up at me and say, 'But Mama,' and I would break into laughter. But you know, talk about empowerment, I don't know that Maxine had ever written a midrash. I keep pushing Maxine to get the midrash she has written since then published because other people need to have them to see it's another way that the scriptures absolutely come alive."

Hard work. Fun. Passion. Empathy. The presenters often learning more than they gave to the participants. The programs from the Spirituality Network have embodied all of these. And everyone who has been a part of them has been blessed.

THE JOURNEY

One day you finally knew
what you had to do, and began,
though the voices around you
kept shouting
their bad advice —
though the whole house
began to tremble
and you felt the old tug
at your ankles
"Mend my life!"
each voice cried.
But you didn't stop.
You knew what you had to do,
though the wind pried
with its stiff fingers
at the very foundations,
though their melancholy
was terrible.
It was already late
enough, and a wild night,
and the road full of fallen
branches and stones.
But little by little,
as you left their voices behind,
the stars began to burn
through the sheets of clouds,
and there was a new voice
which you slowly
recognized as your own,
that kept you company
as you strode deeper and deeper

into the world,
determined to do
the only thing you could do—
determined to save
the only life you could save.

-Mary Oliver

I had finished another wonderful chapter on the life and growth of the Spirituality Network. It seemed that on each page I'd read, one of the participants in the Network-sponsored programs had touched me with their experience. I decided I would ask Jean or Linda if the organization had a newsletter or some other way to communicate information about upcoming programs. I wanted to see what might be offered that would be of interest to me.

I sat the book aside and went for a walk. My mind and spirit had been exercised. Now I needed to bring my body into harmony.

When I returned, the strangest thing had happened. On my front porch was a single yellow rose in a delicate crystal vase. I picked it up and admired its symmetrical beauty then opened the small card attached to the vase. "For your journey," said the simple message. I knew that a yellow rose stood for friendship, joy, and gladness. But I also knew that it stood for freedom, and I chose to accept that meaning. After all, my journey led to the freedom inherent in God's love.

"Now who could have sent this to me?" I wondered. "My friend, Linda, who was encouraging me on this journey? Jean, who had gotten me to take the first steps?" My heart skipped. "Could it possibly had been my husband, Matt, who had started to seem interested in what this was all about?"

I decided I would not ask. I would simply accept the gift as it had been given and savor its beauty as I continued on my journey.

REFRESHING THE WELL

mazingly, with all of its struggles and difficult financial times, the Spirituality Network continued to survive and to meet its goal of bringing hope and spiritual development to the underserved in an ever-expanding community. The organization was truly blessed and was making plans for a Network assembly, bringing together the Coordinating Council, all committee members and the staff at the beginning of its tenth anniversary.

Maxine Shonk extended the invitation: "We are beginning our tenth year as a Network, and we can't wait to celebrate with you all the good work that has been done and the community that is being formed. It is very important to us that you come. As the Network grows in scope and in number, we are doubling our efforts to maintain the vision and connection among us. Please know how we hold you in our heart and prayer with a great deal of gratitude."

Even as the Network prepared to celebrate, financial pressures drove many discussions. All Network members were asked for support, patience, under-standing, creativity, and input to help establish a collaborative and effective organizational structure to carry the Network into the future and preserve and maintain its vision through transitions.

Dick Wood, who had been the lone Protestant on the first Board of Directors, recalls the decision-making process at the Network. "I remember being very impatient to make decisions. I would expand an organization into five states and hire fifteen people in the time it took the Network to make a decision. I learned to love discernment, and I think it stayed with me. I think it was somewhat responsible for us being able to do the things we did."

Noreen says, "Discernment has been one of the biggest struggles as people come into the Network arena. They're more accustomed to an organizational style where somebody is in charge, rather than the Spirit. I know that it seems as though nobody's in charge at times. That's where I always felt the call to believe that the Spirit is in charge of this. I know it was God's grace. Different people would ask me, 'Noreen, where's the master plan?' I would come back with, 'That's the work of the Spirit.' We didn't have a master plan when this thing started. Part of me hopes we still don't have a master plan in our pockets. That we're willing to trust."

If "discernment" was a key word to the development of the Network, so was "collaboration." Noreen explains: "The value of collaboration is in the experience of it. A collaborative structure is built on shared ownership, leadership and responsibility and is fired by shared vision and interdependence. Collaboration empowers people because it depends on each person's contribution to the whole. It fosters diversity and reverences it."

Kerry Reed says, "I loved hearing that because there are so few places where collaborative effort is the primary thing. It's somebody that is going to dominate this gathering or this idea, or it's left up to them to carry through, and then there's all this 'What about collaboration?' and 'How do we do this in a collaborative spirit?' That I think has been, for me, what has probably kept me coming back. It's real life, and we can only do it collaboratively if we're doing it at that level."

Informal conversations with denominational representatives, religious congregations and agencies on collaborative possibilities led to a meeting of the boards of the Ohio Institute of Pastoral Care (OIPC) and the Spirituality Network. Initial conversations centered on the possibility of the Network and OIPC sharing an executive director. While that plan did not work out, the two organizations agreed to continue collaborative efforts on joint programs.

Dialogue on collaboration with religious congregations led the Franciscan Sisters of Stella Niagara to donate the services of Barbara Goodridge, a member of their community, to the Network for 1995–1996. During the time Barbara spent with the Network, she led and expanded the weekly Women-to-Women program at Faith Mission and developed a similar program for men. Barbara also established a new program so the women would have ongoing support after they left Faith Mission.

After a decade of dependence on the Dominican Sisters of St. Mary of the Springs for facilities and a cadre of volunteers for every task that needed performing, there was a strong feeling that the Network needed a permanent space of its own and some paid staff support.

The need for facilities was accelerated when it was learned that a major renovation was planned for Mohun Hall where the Network was housed at St. Mary of the Springs. The renovation would take eighteen to twenty-four months and required the Network offices to move. A long-range question surfaced: Did the Spirituality Network want to be considered in re-allocation of space when the renovation was complete? To explore options for the pressing need to relocate and to look more closely at long-term housing the Board established an ad hoc committee. Committee discussion looked at a return to the Dominican site or a permanent relocation. Reasons for staying included identification with an established institution and greater financial security. A presence in the Dominican facility brought life to the sisters, and the sisters added a unique dimension to the Network's ministry.

Reasons for relocation recognized that the Network struggled with an identification as primarily Dominican or Catholic, which could limit the Network's ecumenical efforts.

Taking a step in faith that they would find the necessary financial resources, the Network named Jeanne Purcell to fill the need for a bookkeeper and Jo Ann Meeks as the "Dwelling Place" coordinator. Her task was to research Network housing possibilities and report back to Council. Jo Ann also led a campaign to raise funds targeted for rent and maintenance for the Network facilities being sought. Jo Ann asked all associated with the Network to donate at least $1 each month on an ongoing basis to help meet the Network housing costs. As part of a new strategic plan, there was a goal expressed for the Spirituality Network to become financially self-supporting, developing a financial structure that would support the Network's ministry. How this objective was to be met was not specifically identified.

With continuing financial support from the Dominican Leadership, the Spirituality Network held an open house in a new home at 762 East Main Street in Columbus on August 18, 1996. Nearly 150 people came to share in the sacred moment. They processed around and through the building on the edge of downtown. There was a recognition that the Network, too, was often on the edges of people's lives — helping all to move toward the center. During the procession through the Network's new home, the group chanted and invited God's Spirit into the space. Silent prayer followed the procession and chants. The open house was a concrete expression of thanks and hope connected with the space.

The program said in part, "Our dwelling place today is the work of a loving God and the result of the care and creativity of many. This new home has been furnished and decorated by the gifts and presence of volunteers, staff and friends—old and new. There are many to thank: the dreamers and shapers, the prophets and preachers who, over these last ten years, have brought the Network to this glorious day of homecoming."

The Spirituality Network was most visibly a 'network' during this time its home was a duplex. The home was a center of hospitality, a comfortable place where many volunteers worked in outreach ministries and gathered for Thursday prayer. Generous creativity and the stewardship of groups and individuals furnished and decorated the dwelling place for less than $500. Noreen remarked at the time, "Our leap of faith has been affirmed beyond our dreams. We trust that your continued generosity through the monthly Dwelling Place Fund will enable us to pay the monthly rent and utilities in order to remain in the midst of the city for a long time to come. It has now come together and it is a wonder to behold. God is good and so prodigal!"

After getting settled in the Network's new offices, Noreen wrote to resource members in September 1996. She said, "One of the most important 'next steps' we need to take in order to insure the Network's future is to begin to chart very closely all the activities in which we are involved. As the Network continues to grow and the need for funding increases, it is wise to track the growth in order to attract funding via grants and other philanthropic sources."

By the end of April 1997 foundational changes were unfolding at the Spirituality Network. The energy and time devoted to examining and refining the organizational structures in conjunction with doing spiritual ministry was taking a toll on Maxine and Noreen. Maxine wrote to the Coordinating Council, "It is with regret and a sense of hope for the Spirituality Network that I submit my resignation as its administrator effective May 31, 1997 with a willingness to transition the position through June 30, 1997."

Maxine explains her decision: "As the Network lives into its vision and into the growing demand for its services, it has become clear to me that there is an increased need for a full-time operations director whose sole ministry is to the administrative details and operations of the Network and whose energy and expertise match the demands of the position. While I know my contribution to the growth of the Network in these six years, my greatest gifts and my training do not lie in the administrative field but in the ministry of spirituality."

Noreen requested a year of transition in her role as coordinator effective June 1, 1997. Noreen proposed to the Coordinating Council that for the following year she would continue her primary focus of "external networking with the wider community, endorsers, organizations, churches, and individuals as a means of promoting the vision of the Network." She also proposed to, "Work with a full-time paid operations director in order to connect the operations of the Network with the vision and mission while removing myself from the day-to-day business of the office."

Sharon Reed, as representative of the Coordinating Council and an active member of the Network from its beginning, wrote the members and friends of the Spirituality Network about the developments: "Spring is a time of powerful transition for our earth and for our spirits. We experience and celebrate the faithfulness of God in rising and springing forth into our world year after year (albeit not always on our timeline!). Thus we come to believe that God is that faithful in all the transitions in our lives . . . change after change, dying after dying, transformation after transformation . . . in the becoming, in the regenerating and in the renewing."

Sharon continued, "We here at the Network are in the midst of our own springtime transitions. After a long process of personal discernment, prayer and consultation, there are several developments that we want to call to your attention and about which we ask you to help us pray." Sharon went on to provide details of Maxine's resignation as administrator of the Network and established the strong need for the expertise and training of a full-time paid replacement. Sharon said the Coordinating

Council had begun the search for an operations director for the Network and encouraged members and friends of the Network to let qualified and interested people know about the search.

In her letter to the Network members, Sharon also addressed Noreen's situation: "Noreen will continue as coordinator of the Network until June 1998, to assure a one-year transition and to secure a financial foundation. She will have as her primary focus the external networking with the wider community, promoting the vision of the Network, and working with the operations director to connect the operations with the vision and mission while removing herself from the day to day business of the Network offices. In the spring of 1998, a search committee will be appointed to identify Noreen's replacement." Noreen's health had plagued her off and on, and she felt the need to pull back from the demands of the growing Network.

Help would soon arrive. Noreen welcomed Anne Rapp to the position of operations director. She said Anne brought a wide range of gifts and particular skills in verbal and written communication to the role. Noreen noted, "A special challenge to this position is grasping all the many facets of the Network and especially getting to know the more than two hundred members." Anne, who had served as a volunteer and who regularly attended programs offered by the Network, had a running start.

"I think what impressed me from the very beginning," Anne says, "is the faithfulness of the volunteers. I hate to start mentioning names, because I know I will leave so many out. I was particularly impressed with Sister Frances Gabriel. Here was a Dominican nun in her eighties who had taught herself the computer and was proficient enough to be of good help. Sister Tillie Vaitekaitis, another Dominican, was not averse to any chore that needed doing. She would take on the most menial tasks: cleaning toilets, mopping up spills, wiping down tables. If it needed doing, Tillie did it. Jane Brockman, Marilyn Larkin, Theresa Devitt. These were women who all had families and other commitments, but they were extremely devoted to the Network's needs. Corrine Hughes starting coming every Thursday when I was operations director, and to my knowledge, she volunteers on Thursday to this day. What a gift these women were . . . and men like Roger Harris. I can't forget Roger."

With an operations director in place, it was time for another letter from Noreen. She was in a reflective mood after reading an article in *SOJOURNERS*. A question in the article struck a chord: "Shouldn't we act as if we believe the unlikely promises of God?" Noreen said she asked herself "What keeps me from such radical belief?" She had a grocery list answer, which was followed by another question. "What helps me believe when everything is in chaos?" She thought for a moment. "For now," she wrote to members, endorsers, participants, volunteers and staff, "my answer is extremely simple: YOU! YOU who are the heart of the Network. YOU help me believe that this dream we call the Network is one of God's unlikely promises, and that God is going to keep this promise!

It is YOU who give me hope for the future as you give so generously of your time, talent and money. God WILL keep this unlikely promise of the Spirituality Network alive because of YOU and your radical faith in a God who never breaks a promise!"

762 E. Main St., Columbus, Ohio
The Spirituality Network's Place of Welcome

SHEDDING THE CHRYSALIS

We were told at the beginning: Expect
    everything to change!
Pulse raced, face tightened,
spirit screaming, "NO!!"
Now I survey all the leave-takings, the
    spent brown husks;
chrysalis, or wrap of daffodil, husk of
    Resurrection.
Dream-figures called to me in the night,
    giving tale, questions —
I chose new companions to listen with
    me.
Homey working-class church, there for
    me in the desert times,
changed for a new home of loose and
    joyful worship.
I emerged from the chrysalis need of
    summer wind, of green
and the scent of blossoms.
There is sadness in the drying of wings,
    beating fresh life,
sadness at the loss of security, tight
    brown husk
that passed for peace. There are friends
    who are memories now;
caterpillar-memories; Past, no longer
    Present.
There will be new leave-takings as I beat
    my wings toward the sun,
sad at the husk behind, joyful in the
    freedom
of endless fields of gold.

-Holly Bardoe
Graduate of the 2002 Wellstreams program

WELLSTREAMS

As the Spirituality Network begins celebration of its twentieth year of serving a thirsty community, the Wellstreams program has reached its tenth anniversary. For many, Wellstreams is what has brought them to the Spirituality Network. Wellstreams is described as a two and a half year ecumenical program of spiritual formation and training in the art of spiritual direction. The Wellstreams brochure explains the meaning of its name this way:

> *Into the calm of life there often falls an unexpected stone of awareness. While sinking to unfamiliar depths of discovery, it also stirs up the clear refreshing waters within. This water cannot be contained but insists on streaming out in a life of thanksgiving and compassion. The Wellstreams program honors in each individual this ever-deepening cycle of awareness and empowerment.*

This description is in total harmony with the ripple effect illustrated in the Spirituality Network's logo.

Although more than ten years old now, the roots of Wellstreams go much deeper. In fact, all the way back to the early days of the Spirituality Network. In September, 1992, the Network was in the process of moving from an Advisory Board to a more traditional, hands-on board. Carol Ann Spencer, a Dominican sister, was just returning to Columbus from a sabbatical in 1992 and was tapped to be the first president of the board. Carol Ann explains her management approach: "The only way that I knew how to have a working board was to have committees that were active and doing the work. I ended up chairing the education-formation committee on top of being board president." The primary purpose of the committee was to study the feasibility of starting an ecumenical training program for spiritual directors in central Ohio.

Carol Ann's committee was a talented one with highly recognized credentials in spiritual direction, including graduates of the Institute for Spiritual Leadership program in Chicago; the Shalem training program in Washington, D.C.; the Archdiocese of Los Angeles training program; the Center for Spiritual Direction in Bird Island, Minnesota, Creighton University; the Graduate Theological Union in Berkeley, California, and the Jung Institute in Geneva, Switzerland. Several had seminary training in the Catholic, Methodist, and Lutheran traditions.

The committee members brought a variety of experience to the dreaming and planning sessions. Carol Ann says, "Early in our discernment we envisioned our training program in two phases, which I now believe form the cornerstone and distinctive mark of Wellstreams. We decided that it was both a spiritual formation and spiritual direction program that we wanted."

At the first meeting in 1992 the committee members began to get to know one another by sharing their stories. They also left the meeting with an assignment. Each committee member was asked to come to the second meeting with their personal definition of spirituality and spiritual direction, and they were also asked to describe their idea of a formation program.

The visions of a training program were as varied as the participants' personal experiences. The definitions of spiritual direction covered a broad range, too. The shortest definition was, "Spiritual Direction — to assist others in following the leading of the Holy Spirit." A more developed definition was, "Spiritual direction is primarily the work of the Spirit. It is an interpersonal relationship in which one person companions another in listening to God's voice in everyday experiences of one's life."

After spending three years chairing the committee that planned the program, Carol Ann found that she had become a believer and was excited enough to apply for the position of director. Once she was named the director of Wellstreams, she had only about three months to get ready for the first group of nineteen journeyers scheduled for January, 1996.

"I used to tease the first group, 'Well, I guess you're our guinea pigs,'" Carol Ann says. She adds, "But I think they got a good program. Each year, each time, we've tweaked it and continue to try and grow it. I think we have good quality supervisors and that's what makes the program."

A hope was expressed that programs would be open to everyone, including the poor and disadvantaged. There was a desire for the inclusion of African Christianity/Spirituality. One proposal called for a three-phase program: the first open to anyone wanting to grow in faith and self-knowledge; the second phase open to those exploring the call to spiritual direction; and the third-phase participants would be supervised while engaging in spiritual direction ministry. In many ways this is a good summary of what the Wellstreams program has become. In 2004, Wellstreams expanded to include an alternative tract for those wanting spiritual companioning training. Inclusion of the second tract led to twenty-four people joining the 2004 class, the largest in Wellstreams' first ten years.

Early discussions during formation of Wellstreams centered on the language that would be used to describe the program and teach the course content. Some on the committee pointed out that words such as 'discernment,' 'spiritual formation,' and 'spiritual direction' are most distinctly Roman Catholic terminology. There were many examples of how the language referring to the spiritual life differs among groups. Carol Ann remembers: "People will call up and express interest in the training program. We'll say to them, 'Are you in spiritual direction?' And they'll answer, 'No.' In talking with Kerry Reed, he said that, in many instances, Protestant denominations have a kind of spiritual direction but they don't use that term. I know that in the Afro-American tradition there is a mentoring that happens that is like spiritual direction companioning, but they would never use that term." The group knew that in order to broaden the base beyond the Catholic tradition, they would have to pay attention and carefully define the language.

The first year of the program was a time for discernment, helping participants determine if they had the gift for spiritual direction. The committee believed the foundational courses would create common ground for people with diverse backgrounds and varied educational experiences and decided not to require an academic degree. In the first year, participants worked with two questions: What does this material say to me about my own faith journey, and what does this have to do with the ministry of spiritual direction? All of the first year courses were seen as fifty percent content and fifty percent process. Carol Ann says, "Part of my own philosophy of spiritual direction is that ninety percent of what I need to be a good spiritual director is to be faithful to my own spiritual journey, and the other ten percent are tools and skills that can be taught and enriched."

Each of the first year participants were uplifted, some in ways they never expected. Kay McGlinchey counts herself in that category. She is a mother, a grandmother, and a minister at Gender Road Christian Church in Canal Winchester. "We were 'forced' to go on a silent retreat at the end of the third semester of Wellstreams, and I went kicking and screaming at the thought of doing nothing and being silent. I received a huge emotional healing and have never missed a yearly silent retreat since. It is food and nourishment for the soul — alone time with God. I have always tried to be open to God's leading, even in the unknown, and Wellstreams was a blessing beyond any expectation."

With a brand new program like Wellstreams, once Phase One was underway, the leadership was working hard to stay one step ahead of the participants as they planned for Phase Two. Jane Belanger was one of the leaders. "I had just finished a spiritual direction training program in Minnesota. I was setting up shop, if you will, in this area and I realized the Network was a resource." Jane joined the faculty of Wellstreams, teaching a prayer course with Kerry Reed and was tapped by Carol Ann to enter training to be a supervisor.

"During that first year," Carol Ann says, "we gathered about ten experienced directors, and we began a self-formation program to prepare us for the role of supervisor in Phase Two. We had little hands-on experience of supervision, except for our own."

"I was in on that," Jane remembers. "We critiqued ourselves and taught ourselves how to be supervisors. I think the actual preparation part of the supervisors was at least a year."

Whatever the training technique that was employed, it was effective, meeting the need to prepare the supervisors for the next stage schedule. The first year's classes ended with a discernment retreat, and seventeen participants (two dropped out in the first semester) requested admittance to Phase Two. All were approved.

Since the Wellstreams program was designed to help participants be faithful to their own spiritual journey, it is important that participants be willing to engage in the personal interior process necessary for growth and development. It was exactly what Karen Herrmann was looking for. She was volunteering within the Network's Women-to-Women program when she decided to pursue a degree in counseling. Twenty years earlier she had taken a class in spiritual direction and was interested in obtaining further training but did not think she could go to Chicago to train, given that she had a husband and children. "So when the Wellstreams program began," Karen says, "I did not hesitate to apply. I was in the first group who had the opportunity to go through the formation process of spiritual direction. My experience with the Network and Wellstreams was a stepping stone to finding the path of my life."

As Karen continued to listen to what was unfolding in her life, she felt led to pursue advanced training in analytical psychology, continuing her studies at the Jung Institute in Zurich, Switzerland. Today Karen is in private practice in Columbus.

In Phase One, each Wellstreams participant has an assigned mentor. The mentor is not easy to define because no one word captures completely the relationship. It is a relationship between two mature adults who value and respect each other, who share common interests and concerns, who enjoy the company of one another, who can rejoice and grieve together, and who can accept, support, challenge, and trust one another. Phase Two is where the Wellstreams program builds on the foundational courses and introduces participants to the practice of spiritual direction.

Kay McGlinchey says, "I had never even heard the words 'spiritual direction' before and, of course, one of my first assignments was to get a spiritual director. Well, that was one of the most healing things I have ever done. I have had two different wonderful spiritual directors, been in group direction with my peer group, which has been an extraordinary experience, and now I have the privilege of being a spiritual companion myself. It has been an awesome process and such an asset to God's ministry for me in the church."

Sharry Hoch is another Wellstreams graduate who was profoundly moved by her experience of spiritual direction. "I first heard of the Spirituality Network in 1990 when I attended a parish women's retreat facilitated by Loretta Farmer and Sharon Reed," she says. "When they mentioned spiritual direction, I leapt at the opportunity to meet with Loretta on a regular basis. It filled a void that had plagued me for a long time – the need to hear a woman's perspective on spirituality and to be affirmed for my efforts to be faithful to God, family, work, and parish. Loretta encouraged me to listen to the Spirit within myself and to act on it, while giving others the freedom to do the same."

After fifteen years of experience with Network spiritual directors, Sharry was led to participate in the Wellstreams program. "The comprehensive program brought about a whole new phase of my spiritual journey," Sharry says. "It has given me the direction and confidence to share with others what I have received from the Network all these years."

Barb Davis from First Community Church entered the training program in 1997 and praises Wellstreams for illuminating the way life experiences, conversions, bring change; we experience transformation by being in a liminal space. Barb sees the process as an almost painful, or at least wrenching, experience. Likewise the Network has had multiple rebirths, and Barb believes it is important to share the struggles and frustrations of this labor-intensive happening.

Barb says, "I've found a home and have been recognized as hungry for God." Barb has become a spiritual director while continuing simultaneously to be involved in her own spiritual direction.

Michael O'Brien worships at the Newman Center in the campus area of The Ohio State University. He is a graduate of the fourth Wellstreams class and uses the same analogy to describe his experience. "Going through the Wellstreams program was a sort of home-coming for me. I felt like I belonged there, and all in the program helped put "flesh" on that which had been calling me. It was, and still is, an invitation, a challenge and a privilege to 'Take the Road Less Traveled' and companion another fellow traveler up the path to where the air is freer and the view is spectacular. I bless them and am forever grateful to those gifted spirits who encouraged me and pointed the way."

The fifth and final semester of Wellstreams formation involves a Synthesis project. It's one of the last things the students do in the final semester. "It's not a paper," Carol Ann says. "We only want a brief explanation, so we ask that they capture in poetry or art what the journey of the two and a half years has been like for them. And some of the projects have been very powerful."

Each one reflects on and integrates a personal journey, pondering where this journey leads. Wellstreams students are asked to be as honest and as vulnerable as possible and given free reign to express themselves in whatever media they choose. Creativity is encouraged. The outcome of the Synthesis projects has had great variety. Participants have used poetry, music, art, pictures, words, and images to express what has happened to them in the formation process. It is each person's summary and integration of who they are and what spiritual direction is for them as they reach the end of this part in their individual journey. The

Synthesis project helps participants express their core values and discern if there is a call to spiritual direction or a related ministry.

Dan Schleppi, a member of the 2004 Wellstreams class, chose photography as his medium of expression. Photography had long been a hobby of Dan's, but he was without a camera. He'd lost it when his home was robbed. At a community-wide garage sale one day, he felt Spirit-led to a particular driveway that appeared to have only baby and kitchen items. Resting his hand on what he thought to be a diaper bag as he looked around, he was surprised to be asked if he was interested in the camera. The bag was filled with the same type equipment he'd lost, and Dan knew he was meant to begin taking pictures again.

When Dan entered the Wellstreams program, the camera was with him. On his retreat, he began taking pictures of images that spoke to him and continued to use the camera on his journey. When the Synthesis project was announced, Dan knew why he'd been taking so many photos. All of the photos he presented were taken in the last year of Wellstreams.

Dan says, "All my time and introspection while in the Wellstreams program seems to have reawakened my desire to create." The lead photo in Dan's reflections from his journey is called "Guide and Traveler."

Guide and Traveler

Guide and Traveler

Guide and Traveler find themselves in this
    location of holy space. They
arrive quite by choice; not because they chose
    the destination, but because
they chose to explore the journey. They chose
    to...
...look beyond the darkness.
...seek deeper truth.
...find a greater understanding of God.
...look at the patterns that ripple through
    our lives.
...find light in the darkness.
...travel in the dark and wet to find the
    hidden beauty there.
...see what lies locked away that needs to be
    allowed to die away.
...slow down and take a closer look.
...find beauty in the old and the ordinary.
...enter the darkness.
Guide and Traveler embark on discovery
    of the journey together. As the
discovery unfolds, the traveler may
    find...
...reflections of the life around them.
...a new viewpoint for what was thought
    to have already been seen.
...kindred souls to share parts of the
    journey.
...beauty in the ordinary.
...greater meaning in the familiar.
...the familiar in a new light.
...patterns superimposed on patterns.
...things from the past that need revisited
    on a new level.
...things in the woods before unseen.
...new meaning in life.

For the Wellstreams program leaders, the Synthesis project also embodies the hope that this reflection will enable the participants to integrate further their previous life experiences with their experiences in Wellstreams.

Janice Bachman is a faculty member for the Wellstreams program. In early 1998, Janice became coordinator of spiritual directors for the Network. She appreciated opportunities to get to know the spiritual directors and become familiar with their individual styles and focus as she tried to match those seeking direction with directors. "I see spiritual direction as a sacred trust in which another entrusts their sacred story to me. Oftentimes, I find myself holding their story, reflecting it back to them so they can see it more clearly, calling even more into their awareness, as we both contemplate what they are verbalizing from their own experience. We are both looking at what God is doing in the stuff of our everyday lives. And, I, as spiritual director, am always changed by the experience of listening to each person.

"Spiritual direction is a graced experience," she continues, "and the Network has raised the awareness of so many in the Columbus metropolitan area of what spiritual direction is. And, the spiritual direction training program, Wellstreams, is a great resource for the Columbus community."

Some of those who participated in the Wellstreams program share the impact of that experience:

> *Jeanne Purcell:* "I participated in a year of the Wellstreams program. It kept bringing me back to that inward journey of finding

God within and finding out who God really created before all that garbage. That's a journey we take through our whole life. I was very happy in the discoveries and the epiphanies, meeting God there. It was just a holy space."

Martie Schoener: "The Wellstreams program has touched my life in places and ways that will stand forever changed. Perhaps my most profound understanding has been that most of us, in some way, try to contain or limit God according to our own narrow vision. It is through my experiences in Wellstreams that I have come to cherish my experience of God in all things – people, places, and events. Even in the very chaos of my own life – the places I once believed God couldn't be. I now have the freedom to accept that there is even a piece of God living and breathing in me!"

Cheryl Lynch Simpson: "When I embarked on the two and a half year Wellstreams program, I expected to learn a lot about the art and science of spiritual direction, but I did not expect to be changed in the process. Wellstreams is more than a certificate program about a growing spiritual practice, it's a formation program that molds participants into the shape God desires for them, the shape God knows will allow each participant's giftedness to be most completely poured out into a needy world."

Holly Bardoe: "On the very first Wellstreams opening retreat for our class, one of the soon-to-be-graduated members of the previous class told us that we could expect everything in our lives to change. On hearing this, I became afraid. I usually shrink from change, immediately assuming the change will be for the worse. The most momentous change is in my relationship with God. I realize now that, as a human being, I am a Mystery within a Mystery, and so is every other creation on the planet! Life cannot be lived by endlessly figuring everything out. For the more I try to do that, the more Mystery is hidden from me. I have received much knowledge of great value in my time in Wellstreams, but the greatest knowledge is that so much will remain unknowable. And this is a source of great joy!"

Judy Niday, CPPS: "Life offers many opportunities for growth. I found myself wondering what I was going to do with the rest of my life. As a preschool and primary teacher who loves to learn, I knew there was more for me to learn about myself in relationship with others and my God.

Wellstreams offered me a wonderful playground where I could experience new learning. Various forms of worship, personal prayer, and dialogue with spiritual directors and supervisors provided new growth for me. It meant letting go and being open to new ways of paying attention to God in places I hadn't thought to look, let alone experience. For to embrace who I am, whole and entire, is to develop a listening heart for another's spiritual journey."

Sharry Hoch: "I entered the Wellstreams program with great anticipation of the spiritual knowledge I would gain. I'm leaving the program with the stunned realization that spiritual growth, as well as the art of spiritual direction, is not accomplished as much by gain as by loss. And these past two and a half years have been mostly about letting go and letting God. It's a fearful thing to fall into the arms of the living God, and also into the Wellstreams program. A really awesome thing!"

Donna Menigat: "The companionship of others on a spiritual journey greatly enhanced the classes. There is little that can compare with the experience of being with kindred souls on a desired and similar learning trajectory. The journey continues as each of us begins to use our knowledge and skills in our present lives. Some of us are seeking new paths; others are incorporating the learnings into aspects of our current lives."

Because of the support and involvement of the Dominican sisters of St. Mary of the Springs, the beginning class of Wellstrems was heavily Catholic. However, there have been several classes where Catholics have made up less than twenty percent of the group, and that can be seen as a sign of success in efforts to be more ecumenical. The first Wellstreams group was seventy-five percent Catholic, but the second class had fewer than twenty percent. The third class had eleven graduates, six were Catholic and five were from various denomination. The current class of twenty-four is about twenty percent Catholic, with the rest being members of other Christian denominations, such as Methodist, Lutheran, and Episcopalian.

The Wellstreams program continues its efforts toward maintaining a diverse and ecumenical group of seekers and to attract more men, since, to this point, there have been considerably more women than men completing the program. The program changes in subtle ways from class to class. Carol Ann says, "I don't think we've ever gotten to the point – and I hope we never do – where things are so settled that we don't tweak the program. With the new class we are going to offer an optional sixth semester, which will be pay-as-you-go. The group won't graduate until June 2009, which feels a little better than finishing in January. I've always wanted a sixth semester, and I've always held back because expense-wise it takes you over the top." This sixth semester will be open to graduates from previous Wellstreams classes as well. It will be a continuing education process. Carol Ann says, "Our God continues to bless this ministry with wonderful individuals who yearn for spiritual formation and development and have a desire to companion others on their faith journeys."

After graduating from Wellstreams in 2002, Martie Schoener said it was difficult to put into exact words the impact of the two and a half years. "Significant, profound, essential, life-giving, transforming. It was all of those, and yet, somehow it was more. The word 'gift' comes to mind. Each person in my class was a tremendous gift to me, a revelation of the many faces of God! The Holy One was so graciously and abundantly present in our shared experience. Our great diversity became a woven tapestry of the human experience. I can honestly say that I never in my life felt as loved and affirmed for who I am as one of God's children as I did in the Wellstreams program. It truly was a safe place for each of us to discover more of the 'true self.' This is indeed, a gift beyond all imagining."

When Loretta Farmer first discovered the ministry of spiritual direction, she shared it with her husband, Gary. He wasn't nearly as enthusiastic. He'd spent time in a Catholic seminary and discouraged his wife's intention to meet with someone monthly for spiritual direction. His memory of spiritual direction was meeting with a priest who told him what to do.

Loretta convinced him that times had changed. "This was a whole different experience. Your answers are within you, and it's not someone else telling you what to do. Spiritual direction was inviting the answers out of *you*. This was monumental in my personal development. I believe the Spirit's in our hearts. When I see — when I'm present — I know the Spirit's there. There is no need for words. You can feel the energy. The Network is the first place I had the freedom to say, 'That's real,' without people looking at me going 'Yeah, right. That's your imagination.' It's the first place that I was given the green light to use my imagination, the gift of it, rather than squelch it. The Network gave me, and everyone involved, freedom to let God come bursting through. This is my passion. There's a passion, I think, in a lot of people in the Network that wants to trust the way the Spirit leads us to God."

After reading the chapter on Wellstreams, I felt I'd begun to understand what spiritual direction was about. I knew I couldn't explain it. Not in concrete terms. I knew it was experiential, with each person taking away something different depending upon their needs and what they brought to the experience itself. My understanding of spiritual direction came from the individual stories of the Wellstreams participants. In my church, we would call that witnessing, and, boy oh boy, what power jumped out of the book from the witnesses I'd just read.

I liked Marti Schoener's and Loretta Farmer's feelings that Wellstreams was a gift. That's what I had begun to realize about spiritual direction. That it was a gift of understanding offered by God as we journey toward unrestricted and overwhelming love. The spiritual directors were companions and helped point out the path during those times when life was difficult and confusing, when there were too many questions and not enough answers. For me, that condition seemed almost permanent in my faith life. I didn't know if spiritual direction was the answer I was looking for, but I could certainly tell that it had been for the women and men who chose to share their experiences with me. I vowed to continue praying for discernment and to take a step on my own by calling Jean and setting up an appointment to talk more about spiritual direction. I wanted to do this now, even before I was finished reading the *History of the Spirituality Network.*

MENDING A LEAKY BUCKET

Abbot Lot came to Abbot Joseph and said,
"Father, according as I am able, I keep my little rule and
my little fast, my prayer, meditation and contemplative
silence, and according as I am able, I strive to cleanse
my heart of thoughts. Now what more should I do?"
The elder rose up in reply and stretched out his hands to
heaven and his fingers became like ten lamps.
He said, "Why not be totally changed into fire?"

—Legends from Desert Fathers

Organizations that have been built from the ground up — this would include businesses as well — seem to reach a crisis point when the founder leaves. Noreen Malone did not want her departure to be an impediment to the hard-won progress of the Spirituality Network. That's why she gave her notice a year in advance and worked tirelessly with the board, staff and volunteers to identify a successor. Through prayer and determination, she wanted the Network to continue its ripple of spiritual growth and development to the thirsty base of journeyers. Despite her efforts, the path ahead would prove to be one of the most painful and difficult periods in the Spirituality Network's existence.

After narrowing applicants for the position of executive director to five and coming to an agreement on a financial and benefits package, on June 1, 1998, the Coordinating Council unanimously accepted the search and finance committees' recommendation. Christine Amy was the new executive director of the Spirituality Network.

Chris was a bright and energetic young woman with a bachelor's degree in Religion/Psychology and a masters in Higher Education Administration from The Ohio State University. She had been working at Columbus State Community College, first as a counselor, then alumni coordinator and most recently as coordinator of leadership training. Chris says a realization that God was calling her to something different led her to Noreen Malone to talk about retreat centers. She thought she might want to run or work in a retreat center someday. Instead, Noreen suggested she apply for the executive director's position at the Spirituality Network.

Chris would begin her duties on July 1, with a transition team named to assist her integration into the Network. Michael Jupin agreed to lead a fall Financial Appeals Campaign in an effort to raise forty to fifty thousand dollars, an amount needed to counter the projected deficit for the fiscal year and provide necessary operating capital. The Spirituality Network was beginning a new chapter.

Chris talks about those early days of her tenure as executive director. "When Marge Fenton agreed to be board chair, that was transformational, no doubt about it. She had no idea what she was stepping into. But the business skills that she brought, the honesty that she brought . . . Marge was the one who jumped in feet first. She had great ideas and a lot of energy. Unfortunately, we burned her out, or she would say she burned herself out. But she was transformational, too. If I, on a personal level, had not had her, I would have lost my mind because she was the only one I could call. I didn't know this, but anybody who's been in a director's position, especially at a small organization, knows it's very lonely. You think that you're surrounded by support and you are . . . and then there's that point where you can't talk about things. It's not about being vulnerable; it's about professionalism. That was a hard struggle for me. Marge was a board chair who cared so much, knew so much and really jumped in so much, that I had somebody I could call and say things when there was nowhere else to say them. She just listened. It wasn't about solving everything, although she solved an awful lot of things for us."

After only six months in her new position as the Network's executive director, Chris began to feel some heat. Financial issues had been foreseen, but not resolved at the time of Chris's hiring. Major changes in staffing and in other budget areas were necessary. Chris says, "The money started running out, and like any organization, everybody has to do everything. The finance committee chairperson sat down with me probably the second or third week I was here and went over the budget with me, and I almost ran back to my former position as quick as I could."

Instead Chris took action. The Network created a revisioning team, and Chris asked everyone on the Spirituality Network mailing list, "Are you interested in being transformed, 'changed into fire?' If so, please join us as we, too, are challenged to become like fire, to take risks and step out in faith as we try to follow God's call for the Spirituality Network."

Friends of the Network were invited to an Open Space Revisioning Retreat and asked many questions. It was a working situation, no frills, just people with a strong interest in the Spirituality Network gathering to get something done. Participants were asked to name an issue of interest or concern for the Network. Over a dozen interests were identified and discussed. There were more than fifty people who participated in the retreat and on the teams that met for months following the retreat.

One of the issues discussed was the Main Street location of the Spirituality Network. Rent for one year at that location equaled the Network's deficit. There was agreement the Network needed an office with some rooms and space that would say, "This is a place of welcome." "This is a coming home." Since most Network activities were not site specific, many thought a move away from Main Street would express the concept that the Spirituality Network is the people, rather than a place. Financial reality helped drive that opinion. A move would nearly wipe out the looming deficit.

Chris says, "I still have bad feelings – not regrets because I know we couldn't help it – but some sad feelings about when we had to leave the house on Main Street. It was so drastic. It was very painful for the people who worked so hard to get that house."

Ellen Dunn remembers how thrilled everyone was when the Network moved into Main Street. "It was really wonderful, but then having had that, it's hard to let it go. At the same time there were financial reasons."

There was constant questioning about the right place for the kind of work the Network was doing. Chris says, "We always had choices: downtown, in the suburbs, in a church, not in a church. So we were constantly asking those questions. The instability was hard. It wasn't until after I left, that I realized Noreen had said from day one, this is supposed to be about people. In one sense, even though we constantly struggled, many times we asked, 'What are we about?' 'What do we want to be about?' We were always about relationships. That never wavered. Ever. So we weren't quite as lost as we thought we were sometimes."

Revisioning meeting sessions dealt with Network language, burnout, relationships with churches in Central Ohio and the Network's endorsers, current focus areas and possibly scaling back the focus of actions. In trying to keep the revisioning process alive, the team had determined that the Network needed to focus energies in three specific areas:

1) Expanding systematic spiritual formation opportunities;
2) Improving networking capacities and strategies, (delivering spirituality resources to the community more effectively);
3) Incorporating a commitment to outreach into the larger organization.

Chris explained to the group: "We are going to try to access our collective wisdom, and the wisdom of the Spirit, to discern our call in ministry. We hope to begin to design an organization that embraces our ongoing vision of inclusiveness, community, collaboration, holistic spirituality and outreach to the most vulnerable among us, all in a structure of accountability to our God, ourselves and those we serve."

Friends of the Network were asked to serve on a team and develop a plan to focus on addressing priorities. The co-chairs for the three committees were: Spiritual Transformation – David Hett and Donna Green; Networking – Gwyn Stetler and Carolyn Jurkowitz; Outreach – Teresa Devitt and Barb Davis.

The revisioning team also established the need for a nomination committee for the Coordinating Council and a finance committee needed to develop a balanced and realistic budget for 1999–2000. The team's hard work was taking place as the Spirituality Network was in the process of leaving Main Street and taking up temporary quarters at First Community Church.

Chris says, "One of the most painful parts about having to move that first time to First Community, and having to redesign the staffing was the whole experience with the board. This is realistically when we started to look at the financing line-by-line, and not just put items in because it had been there every year. That's when St. Mary of the Springs withdrew their financial support. They had warned us upfront this is when they were going to cut it off. Going to a board every month – we were often meeting twice a month – and showing them where we were, walking them through that as best I could with Bob McNall's help, and saying upfront as we were planning the next year's budget, 'Here are the choices we have. We cannot afford these full-time people and do this and this and this. We need to look at our priorities.'"

Karen Shepler (board chair when Chris took office) told Chris she always knew how hard Noreen worked for the Network but said she only discovered after

Noreen left how much Noreen also contributed financially to the Network from the stipends she received from her ministry.

Because of Noreen's ministry income and the generosity of the Dominican sisters of St. Mary of the Springs, the Spirituality Network had never had to stand completely on its own two feet. It had never made its own way. The reality of the situation set in.

Chris Amy could see what she was up against. "The transition during those three years was to make the organization understand what it meant to be financially accountable. It was very hard."

The extremely hard parts were reducing an individual's work hours and, in some cases, eliminating positions due to the lack of funds. "I'm sure that anybody who's honest would say those were tough times," Chris says. "They were tough times for staff because the transition involved having to let some people go, and bringing on new people. Changing roles. Some of that was welcome, and some of it wasn't. We were all struggling together. We evolved with it slowly, and that was painful for a lot of us. During that time, staff relationships were just critical to me, the board, the people."

There were board transitions as well. People who could understand the mission were sought. Chris remembers, "We had basically three boards in the three years I was here. The board that I came in under, most of their terms were up soon after I got here. I know it was ongoing. People would change; some would drop off, and we would get others. And that required starting all over again. That's hard. We did a by-law revision during all that time, too."

Chris says that with all that was going on, she was amazed that sanity prevailed. She adds, "But every one of those people touched my life in some way in this organization. They were expected to be hands-on board members. They brought some incredible talents. Gwyn Stetler, a member of the clergy team at Trinity United Methodist Church, brought a whole different mindset to us about asset, capacity enhancement, and openness and inclusiveness. Not that we hadn't had that, but she brought a real emphasis on that for a year or two."

Chris remembers that Gwyn's work at the Interfaith Hospitality Network introduced her and others at the Network to twelve to fifteen women. "Barb Davis and a couple other people and I put together a retreat for the women. We took them to Camp Akita for a day and an overnight. Donna Doone led them in some dance and games and getting-to-know-one-another things. They had massages, and they had time with a spiritual director if they wanted. There was fellowship over meals, and they stayed the night. Never, ever, ever, will I forget the privilege of being there with them. They were amazingly strong women, but they needed care so badly. I've never met people more thankful for that in my entire life. They weren't thankful to me or anyone in particular, but they were thankful for the experience! You could just watch what was happening to them on the spot, the change in them and the relaxation. There were a lot of tears; there was a lot of stuff going on that day." The memory washes over Chris.

She adds, "I will never forget the joy and realizing how little it took for us to make such a difference in their lives. It was also good for me to discover how very much like us they were. Gwyn was good about talking about the 'them' and 'us' type thing. I don't think I knew any homeless people, and I had an image, a stereotype that probably wasn't as extreme as a lot of people have, but it was still a bit of 'I don't know or understand your experience.' After that day, I felt like I did a little better. I'll never know or understand it if I don't experience it. The relationship and the immense change that happened in one day from what seemed like a really simple gift on our part that was so profound for them."

As difficult as her tenure as executive director of the Spirituality Network was, Chris remembers a lot of it fondly. "I think a critical part of the history is the people who came and committed themselves to what-ever period of time that was. I really want to honor that, especially Jeanne (Purcell). Jeanne had been with the Network for I don't know how many years before I came. She was the jack-of-all-trades really; her title was bookkeeper. She saved me when I started here. She was careful about things. She was the hospitality at the house and even at First Community for the time she was there. She was the one that thought of all the things that I was not thinking of, especially when I first got there, about relationships. I was so concerned with learning the job that she really picked up a lot there in building relationships and introducing me to people and explaining to me some of their story and who to include in things. Jeanne was very good at that."

Chris remembers another person she wants to talk about. "Where would we have been without Anne (Rapp)? She was the office manager. Anne along with Jeanne had the gift of hospitality. She knew a lot of the connections of history. She paid really close attention to details, to peoples' stories and relationships. Anne would tell me this person had been in the hospital, and they worked with the Network this long, and then they had this come up in their life. She gave me a lot of history." Chris says Anne protected her. "She was like my mom. If somebody would show up, she would say, 'So-and-so is here to see you. Now here is what you need to know. They were connected with this and they know so-and-so.' Anne kept the Main Street house going, bought all the supplies and kept that household running wonderfully. She was important."

Chris also notes her appreciation for volunteers that helped out in many ways. "Roger Harris started volunteering when Noreen was here. He was critical. When I started, Roger was the newsletter editor. He was the volunteer extraordinaire. He stuck with us – God love that man – through two moves, even though he was up in Sunbury. He always did database stuff. He did our mail merges and newsletter lists and all that until Marianne came. Then he did a lot of database management after that and helped her out. And he would always come in and do other things, too, like work on the copier."

Technology was a challenge for Chris. "I promise you I spent half my time on technology: phones, the copiers, computers and printers. And I don't know anything about those things. So Roger was wonderful."

During the late 90s when a new vision for the Spirituality Network was being birthed, several subgroups of the revisioning team were hard at work. The transformation group explored the following questions:

- ◆ What language is needed to provide inclusion in describing the formation program?

- What other programs of this nature exist in the community?
- How might such a formation program be organized or structured?
- What spiritual needs remain that other Network programs can nurture?
- What partnerships would enhance the mission of such a formation program?

In discussing the definition of spiritual formation and arriving at the concept of *transformation* there was extensive conversation and the desire to be inclusive in word choice. The group came up with the following definition:

> *Spiritual transformation is a journey awakened by the deep yearnings of the heart. This transformation honors in each individual the ever-deepening cycle of awareness and empowerment that gives meaning, value and purpose to life. Spiritual transformation finds its expression both in movement inward and movement outward.*

The committee decided early on that the Wellstreams program was the foundation of the spiritual transformation program they envisioned. Their goal was to offer an expanded Wellstreams program that would attract a broad spectrum of persons "in their common quest for wholeness and integration."

A recurring theme at all networking committee meetings was *mission.* Conversations invariably came back to the existing mission and vision statements. The committee found it impossible to talk about spiritual networking without asking: "In what ways is the Spirituality Network *spiritual*?" and "In what ways is the Network a *network*?" The committee had lots of questions about mission: "Who is the Spirituality Network? Is it an interfaith gathering of people of the Judeo-Christian tradition? Where is God in the Network's mission and in the mission statement? With whom will it network in relationships? Toward what purpose(s) will it network? What spiritual resources, for example, spiritual direction or retreats, will the Spirituality Network network? How will these resources be identified and kept current? To whom will the Network's resources be offered? How are people to access the Network's resources?" There were many questions that needed answers.

The committee adopted the goal of networking to help people in Central Ohio access spiritual resources. The committee felt that throughout the Network's history, networking happened in two ways: first, through service delivery, for example by connecting people with the Network's offerings, whether that meant developing and offering retreats, special programs, speakers for churches, or spiritual direction. The second way the committee felt networking happened was through spiritual resourcing and referral, connecting people with existing community resources. Much of the Network's networking was in direct service delivery.

The outreach team observed that outreach ministry is the foundation of the Spirituality Network; outreach permeates all Network activities and thought. The group said programming and "specific" outreach ministries are unique. These ministries do not have an "agenda," nor is there a set goal to "fix" the problems of those with whom the Network walks. Through companioning and spiritual accompaniment with people struggling with financial, emotional, and/or spiritual issues, the Network is gifted by their courage and their response to adversity as well as their faith and their unique gifts. Network outreach is approached in an "asset-based" manner and does not focus on what is lacking. Network outreach searches for gifts that will empower and reinforce God's presence in the lives of those who are part of the outreach ministry. Goals were proposed for the design and implementation of an outreach training program for new Coordinating Council members and Network members-at-large; and to provide an outreach mentor or minister for Council.

Another goal was to expand the role of the Wellstreams program in outreach ministries and the availability of spiritual direction to the wider community. One way the outreach team thought to address this was by adding an outreach segment to the Wellstreams curriculum.

Other goals proposed by the outreach team were to increase giving directly related to outreach programs in the budget, to utilize current grant monies to carry out retreats for women guests in the shelter system prior to the end of the year, and to develop partnerships with other organizations that might wish to contract with the Network for outreach ministry participation at their locations.

Some of the other suggestions and recommendations made in the revisioning committee were stymied by the finances and the personnel transitions. Even as the committee discussions continued through 1999, the Spirituality Network moved once again, this time to its current offices at First Congregational Church, 444 E. Broad Street in Columbus.

Chris says, "On a personal level, but also organizationally, my two biggest impressions after moving to a new location were transition. I know it was transition across the board. I'm most caught by the physical transitions, because we had to do that twice in three years." Chris shows some fatigue on her face and continues: "Each time – even though it had wonderful results – it was painful. It was physically painful and exhausting. It was a challenge in the sense of keeping our identity and making sure people knew where we were and not losing people just because of the physical changes we were going through."

There were a lot of staff transitions during Chris's three years. She says, "Some of those were wonderful. When we hired Amanda (Stone Cushing) as program coordinator, it changed so much for me in a positive way, because we had been through a lot of leavings by that point either by their choice or, unfortunately, not by their choice. Hiring someone gave me a sense of hope to look ahead." After a pause Chris adds, "It guaranteed us hopefulness that we were going to grow again. My greatest impression is of the relationships, both on an organizational level and personally. I had no idea of the number of people, and the diversity, and the beauty of all the people I would meet in my three years at the Network."

The contribution that each person made at the Network was noted by Chris. "I think each staff person that came onboard was very important. When Jeanne Purcell left, I was in a panic. I did not have a clue how to do what she did. We had two or three volunteers who came in between, but that was not my strength at all. My biggest fear was that I was going to have to do book-keeping. I had enough trouble doing the more philosophical thinking about the budgeting and the big picture thinking without getting into the nitty gritty. I remember the day I met Marianne Reihl. First Amanda came and then Marianne a month or two later. It felt like a continuation of the hope and stability. Besides the bookkeeping, she was wonderful at saying, 'What is this?' No fussing around with her; I loved it. She didn't beat around the bush. That was a great gift. Marianne was wonderful to have because she would ask questions like, 'How?' Carol Ann does that too. 'How are things going to work out?' We need that realistic person who's going to say, 'That's just great, but . . . we need to think some details through.' "

Chris gives Marianne credit for improving the newsletter. "We did a good newsletter before, but she transformed the newsletter. I really think it made a huge difference. Those two skills and bringing her and Amanda on were really pivotal."

While Marianne took care of bookkeeping and the newsletter, Amanda Stone Cushing quickly began developing programs. Amanda, who says she was not raised in a religious family, found the desire to build a closer relationship with God only after she married and her children were born. Following the thirst that resides in all of us, she found her way to the Network and entered the first Wellstreams class. She had worked as a trainer for corporate clients, and when her company went out of business, an announcement that the Spirituality Network was looking for a program coordinator seemed like a call from God.

With three strong women in key staff positions at the Spirituality Network, Chris Amy submitted her resignation in December, 2000. Her two-and-a-half years as executive director at the Network ended January 31, 2001. In the end, Chris knew when her best work was done. "I think the way I look at it, it was definitely a calling *from*. I've been called *to* a lot of things in my life, but that was definitely a calling from. It's just that sense you've done all you can do here right now, both from your ability and the other people's abilities. That is hard to recognize."

Chris remembers that each day she spent at the Network was filled with surprise. "I was always amazed by the people who would just show up. People would walk through that door and say 'I saw your sign,' or 'I heard an announcement,' or whatever, and they would come in and you would start by showing them what we did and giving them a newsletter. Almost without fail, whoever welcomed them would almost always end up sitting with them in the office and hearing their story. The stories were so different. I would go home at the end of the day and say, 'Who would ever have thought today I would share somebody's story who was homeless, or somebody who was religiously homeless, or somebody whose background was so different from mine? Or who was experiencing incredible physical or emotional challenges?' We just never knew who was going to walk through the door. That's what enriched me in those years."

She sums up her thoughts: "We did great things with programs. We did great things with the organization and the strategic planning. But the relationships are what remain with me. I've never worked with better people. I've worked with great people, but never better people. There is no way to thank you all enough for the wonderful companionship and life lessons you have shared with me and the many gifts I have received during my time as director. I have been witness to the most holy moments in so many lives, and feel more than ever that the work of the Network is *vital* to the world, as it has been to me in many ways."

I was sitting in Jean's house telling her how painful it had been for me to read this last chapter on the history of the Spirituality Network. "I think the chapter could have been called, 'Birthing a New Vision,' " she said to me. "We women know that the birthing process is always painful. It's the beautiful result after the process is complete that makes you forget the pain."

I could see that she was right. It had been such a struggle for Chris Amy, at times, as she tried to focus on the reality of the situation and make others see the problems as well. In the end, I marveled at how well she had come through it all. She talked so openly and lovingly about the people who had been part of the process. Those were the things she remembered most when her part in the birthing was complete. And, even along the way, she was not over-whelmed with problems to the point of missing the wonderful things that were taking place around her. I remembered her comments about the event the Network had put on for the homeless women and how touched she was by their response. Even her reaction to people unex-pectedly walking through the Network's door and telling their stories before they left said something profound to me about Chris Amy. This was a sensitive and caring person. A holy woman that the Network was fortunate to have leading it for those three years. I wondered how Sister Noreen had reacted to those difficult years, and I asked Jean about it.

"I never talked to Noreen about it specifically," she said. "Oh, I'm sure it was difficult for her, but she also knew that her time in leadership was past, and she was not one to interfere. Noreen is a person who trusts completely in the process. Who knows God is there even in the messes of our daily lives. I'm sure Noreen did what she has always done. She prayed for the Network and trusted that what would happen would be God's will. And I also know that she made herself available to help out at any time and in any way she was asked."

That answer seemed consistent with what I had learned about Noreen. Jean and I went on to discuss spiritual direction in detail. It was the reason for our meeting, and she could see my eagerness to start that phase of my journey. I left with a smile and a hug and a date for our next meeting.

As I was about to enter my car, something caught my eye in the small park across the street. I closed and locked the car door and strolled to the center of the park. I think I sensed something, more than saw it. Instinctively, I headed to the fenced basketball court. The same big man I had seen a few weeks earlier on my first visit to Jean's house was there again, this time without the earphones. And, unless I was completely mistaken, the small boy, who had been unable to open the gate when I had last seen him, was now on the court with him. Evidently, the boy had been successful in getting the man's attention because the two of them were playing together, the man stopping from time to time to give him a lesson in dribbling the ball. At one point, he lifted the boy onto his shoulder so that he'd be close enough to shoot the ball through the hoop. This touched me deeply to see the man as teacher and mentor to this boy who seemed so eager to learn what he could from someone with talent and experience.

When things seem so dark
And creative thinking goes away
When dreams go "poof"
And those closest don't SEE
It all seems too difficult
To accomplish those goals
That felt so God-graced
And so deeply needed.

What now, Lord?
Are you with us?
With a committee of one or a few
Your work cannot be done.
We need to be refreshed in spirit.
Did we really understand your call?

Bless us with clarity and new hope.
Even though we know in our heads
You are always present in our struggles,
In our hearts we sometimes feel aban-
    doned.
Restore our faith in new beginnings
And energize us in body and spirit.

Lighten up the dark moments
And be clear about what you want.
We ask to be sustained by your love
And tenderly offer it to those around us.

OFFERING LIVING WATER

Building community was always a goal of the Spirituality Network, and many of the programs were designed to do just that. Where possible, the major community-building programs were also fund-raisers, since trying to stay afloat financially was a continuing problem. These activities were generally fun as well. Anyone who has spent any time around the Network knows that it is not made up of dour, holier-than-thou people. It is a group full of love, affection, and humor. Each of the community-building activities was approached with that attitude.

Workshops, initiated early in the organization's development, were an invitation to join in expanding the concept of community to one that was more inclusive. These workshops were developed by M. Scott Peck and brought to the Network by Dick Wood from First Community Church. Kerry Reed, senior pastor at Gender Road Christian Church, Canal Winchester, and Sister Maxine Shonk look at the workshops as the highlight of ecumenical activity in Central Ohio during their time. In 1993, the first year that the Network sponsored the workshops, more than one hundred people participated.

In the workshops, people were encouraged to discover new and better ways to live together. The Network invited individuals and groups to communicate with authenticity, deal with difficult issues, welcome and affirm diversity, bridge differences with integrity, relate with compassion and respect, and to affirm a relationship with God.

The process helped people in many ways. These included coming to know and to share personal lives, crossing boundaries of race, culture, creed, economic status, and diversity; and being more rooted in prayer, non-violence, and passion for truth, peace and to the glory of what it means to be human.

It was hoped the workshops would produce revenue but that was not the end result. The workshops were seen as an ideal means, however, to provide a base for the Network's dream of a community dinner where people of mixed culture, economics, race, and faith traditions would sit and break bread in a celebration of community that crosses all boundaries. The Network Council began to prepare for the project.

First Community Dinner

The concept of a community dinner was born in a conversation between Noreen and Larry Reichley as they traveled together to a parish retreat. The plan that evolved from their discussion was to gather, at a common table, people from as many cultures and economic backgrounds as possible. They proposed a celebration of diversity.

Kerry was enthusiastic about the idea of a community dinner. "We were going to have homeless; we were going to have persons who lived in mansions. We were going to have everybody together, and there was not to be a label in front of us. We were going to be community. It didn't have anything to do with where you were from or what you do or any of that. Then I recall later learning where some of the people were from and what they did and it was like, 'Wow, that's just amazing, at this one table that kind of conversation took place!' That was such an incredible gift. I don't know any group that does that. You sense that what brings you together is much bigger than what separates you.

> This is our dream dinner — the rich and the poor, male and female, people of different races and ethnic backgrounds, people neglected and people who are privileged — all equal in God's eyes and, for this night, all breaking bread and celebrating life together.

Those were the words of Sr. Carol Ann Spencer, Coordinating Council President in 1995–96 as she described, "A Touch of Life, A Splash of Hope." On April 20, 1996, the dream came alive when the Spirituality Network hosted its first community dinner, along with its tenth anniversary.

Cantor Vicki L. Axe of Temple Israel touched the heart of what is common and sacred to each one in the room in her opening invocation. Using the ancient Jewish Havdalah, Cantor Axe invited all to bring the sacred into the ordinary. In explaining the richness of the Jewish word *shalom* as one of welcome, thanksgiving, praise, and reverence, she cited the same richness in the Network's vision statement. With the symbol of spices, she invited the attendees to savor the sacredness of connection with all of creation, with one another, and with the Creator, the Source of it all.

The Network wanted someone special to provide an inspirational and motivational talk for its resource volunteers and the general public. It found an exceptional person in Carl Upchurch, winner of the National Humanitarian Award from Operation Push, who provided just the right *TOUCH* for the evening. After spending thirty days in Los Angeles following the 1992 riots, Upchurch organized the Ministry of Urban Peace and Justice. He called the first national summit for gang leaders and community activists and conducted summits in many cities across the U.S. Upchurch was honored by the first President Bush and appointed to President Clinton's Council on Sustainable Development. He received the Martin Luther King, Jr. Peace Award from the State of Ohio in 1989. Upchurch shared his personal journey from prisoner to peacemaker, touching dinner guests with his story of personal slavery to violence and addiction, and his liberation. Upchurch applauded the Network and those gathered at the dinner for the choice to honor goodness in others.

With drumming and singing, the Imani Dancers, added the *SPLASH* to the evening with sparks of joy and celebration. The energy they generated moved feet to dancing, voices to singing, hands to clapping and people to pure enjoyment.

In choosing to address people's spiritual needs without regard to their particular creed or religion, the Network showed an ability to reach a whole segment of society in a non-threatening way — perhaps in a way that a particular religion or faith expression cannot.

Carol Ann says, "No one else addresses the spiritual needs of the people in this way, especially the inner city people and those who are marginalized by prejudice, economic status or lifestyle."

Noreen adds, "We do not equate spirituality with religion. Spirituality involves each person's own journey and quest for inner truth and meaning in life. In companioning people on the spiritual journey, we encourage them to reverence themselves and others, thereby emphasizing nonviolence as a way of life."

Update, the Network's newsletter, said the Celebration of Community dinner "spoke more eloquently of the vision and dream of the Spirituality Network than any words could."

The first honorees of the Spirituality Network's "Touch of Life" awards were Angela Marie Emrick, CSC (Mount Carmel Health System), Richard Wood (First Community Church), Reverend Karen Shepler (Metropolitan Area Church Council), and Sister Margaret Ormond, OP (Dominican Sisters, St. Mary of the Springs) for significant contributions that made the Spirituality Network dream a reality.

"A Touch of Life, A Splash of Hope," was a major fund-raiser for the Spirituality Network, netting $6,000, and was described as "a very hopeful first effort." The Network hoped it would become 'the annual dinner event' to attend in Central Ohio celebrating humanity, community, and the quest for the God of life.

Two community dinners followed in 1997 and 1998, both with the same theme as the original: "A Touch of Life, A Splash of Hope." Both brought back the same wonderful diversity and delicious food and added a silent auction.

The guest speaker for the 1997 dinner was Rev. Carol Stumme, youth advocate and pastor of St. Peter's Evangelical Lutheran Church. She was also the initiator of "Saturday School," a place of enrichment, community, and safety for neighborhood children. Entertainment was provided by Ron Hope and the Youth Drum Ensemble from Short Stop Teen Center and Pete McClernon and the Voices of the Young, St. Peter's Players, Worthington.

In 1998, Edwina Gateley, internationally know speaker and author of *I Hear a Seed Growing* and *Psalms of a Laywoman*, spoke of her experiences and reflections while working with prostitutes on the streets of Chicago. Entertainment was provided by the "Revival Choir," a combined group from central city parishes (St. Dominic, Holy Rosary/St. John, Saints Augustine and Gabriel, and St. Thomas the Apostle), as well as ISSA, an African dance group. Gwyn Stetler of the Interfaith Hospitality Network was the honoree.

The Spirituality Network
Welcomes You To

A Touch of Life

A Splash of Hope

A Celebration of Community Dinner

Pages 146 to 148: Community Dinner

Lenten Journal

No other marketing or public relations effort has been as successful in introducing the Spirituality Network to congregations or individuals as the *Lenten Journal*. It certainly has been a community builder. Father Vinny McKiernan, a Paulist priest stationed at the Ohio State University Newman Center in Columbus, is the central force behind this yearly publication. He describes its beginnings. "I remember we had an Epiphany party to take care of ourselves after Christmas. I suggested, 'Wouldn't it be great if we all polled the readings that we felt were good and circulated them among ourselves, like quotes from Merton or what have you?' Then we talked about copyright problems with that. So then – I don't know who suggested it – someone said, 'Why don't we write our own for Lent to circulate among ourselves for our own inspiration.' Then Judy Halpate – she was teaching RCIA (Right of Christian Initiation for Adults) at St. Francis, Newark – said, 'Oh that sounds good. I could give that to my catechists.' That's when we thought it might have a wider circulation than just among ourselves."

Vinny makes sure everyone knows that putting out the *Lenten Journal* is a collaborative effort. "We were getting everyone involved in this operation. Father Pat Toner was without an assignment when we first did the *Lenten Journal*, and we brought the text over to him at Our Lady of Peace, and he typed all the text. Mt. Carmel West supplied the total printing, and then we would have to collate. Then we delivered them about a day before Lent. Pat typed it for about two years and then Roger (Harris) took over. Since then it has kind of had a life of its own. Lately Jane Kelsey of the Newman Center has been helping a lot; she does all the typing."

To appeal to a wide number of Christians during the Lenten season, those providing reflections on the daily reading were a diverse group as well. Vinny explains, "What we did the first time was we went according to the Catholic lectionary, and so we had St. Joseph in there and the Annunciation. People who were not Catholics were wondering what that was all about. Now we go just with the Lenten readings. I try to get a balance of Catholic and other Christians, men and women, religious and lay. I try to get people who might have some kind of constituency who might order ten or twenty copies of the journals. We print two thousand journals, and two hundred of those are specially bound for prisoners. That came about through sending some to someone that thought this would be great in prison ministry, so we sent her the extra copies and we learned that they have to be taped and can't have the plastic spiral binding."

For fifteen years of the Spirituality Network's twenty-year existence, the *Lenten Journal* has been aiding the interested traveler along the spiritual journey. The *Lenten Journal* features short reflections by contributors with plenty of space for the reader to write personal thoughts. Its success is unqualified. Vinny explains its staying power, "I think we are unique in that it's still a journal. We don't give people a lot of predigested reflection, or prayers or a spiritual bouquet." Like any journey, the traveler must take the steps to reach a destination.

Ron Atwood, spiritual director and pastor of St. Francis of Assisi Catholic Parish in Columbus, Ohio, provided the reflection for Sunday, February 27, 2005. Choosing among four scriptural passages for the day (Exodus 17:3-7, Psalm 95, Romans 5:1-2, 5-8, John 4:5-

42), he selected John 4:15: "*Sir, give me this water, so that I may not be thirsty.*"

Ron offered the following meditation for reflection on that day of Lent:

Under the noon-day sun of her shame
stands the woman
who carries each of our names—
dry-mouthed from our sins—
thirsting for the fresh, cool water
of forgiveness.

Drawn by our thirst,
we meet the One
who sets us free
from the dry dust
of yesterday's infidelity.

The Lenton Journal

Centering Prayer

The Centering Prayer Program was definitely a community-building activity where a sense of humor was required to turn a negative into a positive.

Thomas Keating is a Trappist priest who has written and taught extensively on Centering Prayer. Chris Amy says, "A fund-raising event was an annual thing, and we were brainstorming around a speaker. I said, 'Let's just go for the gusto.' So I called Father Keating and left a message. Darned if one day he didn't call me back personally, which sent me into total shock. He said, 'I'd like to come.' I said, 'Great,' and he said, 'I'm not charging you anything.' I was stunned."

A group planned a wonderful evening, "Centering Prayer with Thomas Keating," at Bethel United Methodist Church to take advantage of Father Keating's wonderful offer. Chris says, "We had hundreds and hundreds of tickets sold, and we were going to do a silent auction and all sorts of stuff. The day of the talk I was closing on my house, and my dad was having heart surgery. Then about two o'clock in the afternoon, we get a call on the voicemail saying, 'Father Keating missed his flight.' I was on my knees! Well, first I was thinking 'What do we do?' Then I went on my knees asking, 'OK, what is this all about?' And Vinny (Father Vinny McKiernan), who was the first person I thought of, naturally, happened to be free and happily agreed to take Father Keating's place. He came and spoke instead."

Chris is struck by what a wonderful evening it turned out to be. She says, "Your first thought is 'This ruins everything.' We couldn't cancel at that point because people were already on their way from Cleveland and other places. So we had to stand at the door and tell people as they walked in. Only two or three people got mad. What we said to them was, 'He's agreed to come later; we'll do this again. Your tickets will be good; we won't charge you again.' And it was such an awesome evening. You think it's all ruined and it all works out.

"Then on top of that, Father Keating came the next month. So we really had two fund-raisers, and we made almost twice the money as we had at any other fund-raiser. Those are the kinds of things that always happen here at the Network."

Chris says the personal lesson for her was to understand what's really important and what's not. "I think there were a lot of people who got as much out of Vinny and what we did that evening as they would have from Father Keating."

Arti Gras Celebration

The idea for the Arti Gras as a community celebration is credited to Amanda Stone Cushing. "The program committee had been kicking around the idea of a series of Lenten programs around the theme of art and the Spirit when I presented the idea of a single day of programs, a sampling of different artistic expressions that relate to the Spirit," she says. Amanda was disappointed that initially the idea was not that well received by the committee. They weren't sure that people would commit to an entire day. It wasn't until Gwyn Stetler came up with the idea of the program being offered free of charge that the committee agreed to give it a try. Arti Gras was the result, a day of artistic and musical expression to be held on the Saturday preceding the beginning of Lent.

The Spirituality Network has been blessed with the gifts of many talented people. Bobbi Gill is one of them. Arti Gras was the perfect opportunity for her and others with a variety of talents to offer their creativity in hands-on workshops that helped attendees find their own creative expressions.

Since its beginning in 2001, there has been a deep connection between creativity, spiritual growth and justice at the heart of Arti Gras. Each year, Arti Gras — paralleling the Mardi Gras celebration of life's richness in preparation for the desert time of Lent — has focused creative exploration around a specific theme. Arti Gras 2005, for instance, challenged participants to create, express, and explore around the theme of "Art and Social Justice." Participants created powerful expressions of their desire for justice, peace, and wholeness through poetry, writing, work with clay, mixed media, painting, body prayer, music, and chant. The creative experience helped people touch the Creator's energy, the "Divine Artist," who is continually creating and re-creating the world one encounters on the spiritual journey.

Arti Gras 2006 was special in many ways. First, the Greater Columbus Arts Council recognized and supported the project with a grant of $2,000. The selling point for the grant was that the event was open to the public and free. It was a day of mini-workshops on yoga and body prayer, poetry, creative writing, jewelry, and mask making — all the different ways in which the arts relate to spirituality.

The second thing that made Arti Gras 2006 special was the tie in to New Orleans. First Community Church had adopted some displaced families that were staying temporarily in Columbus after escaping Hurricane Katrina. The Network invited them to be part of the celebration, and a woman in one of the families agreed to do a mini-workshop on cooking and healing. That concept moved from "Would you like to cook enough so that everybody could sample the food?" to "How about if I prepare the whole meal, and let's do a New Orleans meal." In return, the Network committed to give a portion of whatever was taken in from the auction and donations as a freewill offering back to the New Orleans community.

Tracey Bolds, who offered to cook the meal, worked for many years in a New Orleans restaurant of famed chef, Emeril Lagasse. Before Arti Gras began, Tracey returned briefly to New Orleans and picked up special Cajun-style seasoning that Emeril donated for the celebration, and she used that to cook jambalaya and other foods native to New Orleans.

According to Amanda, the Spirituality Network originally made a commitment to the Arts Council that ten percent of whatever was taken in through freewill donations and the auction would go back to New Orleans. "In the end, we decided to give a portion of the proceeds (more than ten percent) directly to this family that gave so much of themselves to us, to help in their relocation."

The challenge to create is strong in all of us. When it's done on behalf of those whose voices have been silenced through injustice, poverty, war, or natural disaster, we are reminded that God asks us to take our gifts into the world to help build the kingdom. Rev. Tim Ahrens said in his 2005 keynote address, "I have witnessed God's handiwork. It has created a deep peace coupled with a deep discomfort. It has created a zeal to walk humbly, love steadfastly, and to do justice and, — by the way — justice, like art, can only be done, not talked about!"

*Above: A table display of art created
during the day.*

*Below: On the silent auction table —
a beautiful handmade quilt by Barb Davis*

Above: Mo Meuse and Kay McGlinchey creating their art

Below: Arti Gras exhibit

Arti Gras: Popular jazz bandleader
Arnett Howard ready to make music
with Dr. Terry Davis and his famous gutbucket

REINFORCING THE WELL

Following Chris Amy's resignation in December 2000, Network board members called for a time of discernment and transition. In the Spring 2001 newsletter, Gwyn Stetler issued the invitation on behalf of the board: "Together we can honor and learn from the Network's history as we allow it to transform," she wrote.

The transition team brought together the board and staff with Sister Noreen Malone and Chris Amy, the two women who had directed the Network. Gwyn says, "Each time I heard them speak, I was awed by their unique blend of gentle wisdom and entrepreneurial spirit. In their own ways, each has been a trailblazer. To each we owe gratitude."

To honor the two women's work and the spiritual thirst in Central Ohio, Gwyn hoped people would join the Spirituality Network as it discerned a future, both spiritually grounded and fiscally plausible. In presenting a plan for the transformation process, Gwyn quoted Angeles Arrien, award-winning author, anthropologist and educator: "Show up. Pay attention. Tell the truth. Don't get too attached to the results."

- **Show up.** "Now, more than ever, participate. Please, connect as you are able."
- **Pay Attention.** Gwyn requested prayers and encouraged Network members to learn with the board.
- **Tell the Truth.** Gwyn said, "I want to hear your hopes, dreams and blessing for the organization. Your communication and feedback are welcomed."
- **Don't get too attached to the results.** Gwyn said, "If we are truly open to transformation, we know the process is so much more than we can ever imagine.

"Together, may we strive for the Network to emerge even nearer to the heart and intentions of God."

Many questions came up during the discernment. Two of the questions the group returned to repeatedly were, "What do we need to hold on to?" And "What do we need to let go of?" Kathy Klamar, board chair, said there were several things that became clear. "We want and need to hold on to the contemplative tradition and process that was born out of our Dominican heritage. We also want and need to hold on to our emphasis on spiritual direction and training. We need to let go of organizational paradigms that are no longer effective for the Network. This is where much of our challenging work for the year ahead begins."

The board revisited the Network's vision statement and adopted the following: *The Spirituality Network is rooted in the contemplative Judeo-Christian tradition and is dedicated to fostering and awakening spiritual growth through spiritual direction, retreats, and training.*

Kathy said, "While a new organizational design may be a year away, we will not be in a holding pattern for the next year. The board will work at narrowing our focus to that which we do best. We are dedicated to do all that we can to find and mobilize the resources that will help our staff do their jobs well."

Through nearly a year of research, evaluation, and struggle that ended in May 2002 the organizational design team produced six guiding principles for operation of the Spirituality Network. These principles were intended to provide clarification to the Board of Directors and the staff in future planning. Jim Long, the new board chair, presented the guiding principles and stressed the board's commitment to them at the annual meeting in August, 2002:

1) God, in calling us to this ministry, provides the very gifts and resources necessary to fulfill it. Voluntary or evangelical poverty is not a rejection of wealth, but a choice for utter dependence on God.

2) A home is necessary for continued sense of identity and connection to each other and the community. The physical space can be simple, yet provide for administration, staff and volunteers as well as networking and resource activities.

3) A storyteller incorporated into the structure and fabric of the Network's organization — activities and relationships will carry the memory of and for the group. The storyteller perpetuates the mission of the Network.

4) Those who represent the Network on its board and staff should be in spiritual direc-

tion themselves. The core work of the Network is companioning others on their spiritual journeys, so while spiritual direction should not be mandated, it will be strongly encouraged for those in leadership roles.

5) Our desire for God, and God's desire for us, must be the determining factor in all our choices for ministry. All programs, events, ministries, and decisions should be determined through prayerful discernment.

6) We must model contemplative living in all our programs and relationships. Collaborative decision making and prayerful discernment will be the basis of all our processes and relationships. We must model these contemplative practices in all that we do as an organization.

In his first year leading the Network board, Jim and board members took time each meeting to study a guiding principle. Living into the first principle, "utter dependence on God," remained a challenge as bills had to be paid. The difference between the dream and the reality continued.

Despite having the organizational design team's guiding principles, the board struggled to see where the Network was headed. There were board retreats in 2003, 2004, and 2005. Part of the board retreat process was to conduct a SWOT analysis of the Network, looking at Strengths, Weaknesses, Opportunities, and Threats. This process included suggested goals and action steps that grew out of the reflection. There were similarities in goals identified in each of the board retreats. They covered relationships with churches, funding sources, the Network's history, spiritual direction education, and formation.

Above all, there was a recognition that the executive director role needed to be filled so that all staff would have specific areas of responsibility and could be held accountable for fulfilling them. There was a recommendation that all goals should include regular reports to the board and timelines for completion.

Barb Davis became chairperson of the Spirituality Network board in 2004. While reaffirming the Network's roots, she quickly pointed to the future path of the organization. "We connect people thirsting for spiritual growth with our spiritual directors, ever developing our outreach. We know there is great potential to form more relationships with area churches and to offer special workshops and retreats. To fulfill our mission requires financial resources – resources to bring the Network to people, to let people know the Network exists for them. From the outset it has been a challenge, but also the recognition that 'If it is of God' it will happen."

Under Barb's leadership the Network board began an active search for an executive director, but the Network's precarious finances made discussion of hiring someone a difficult topic. In some ways, the resignation of the Network bookkeeper, Marianne Reihl, made the discussion necessary. Marianne's departure meant a new bookkeeper was needed, but the question was explored in a broader context. What else was needed for the Network to generate new energy? What else was needed to enable staff to have clarity around their roles?

Clarity was something that was sorely needed. When Chris Amy resigned, the staff was left to carry on without her day-to-day leadership. Amanda Stone Cushing felt most affected by the situation, as she was a relatively new staff member. The uncertainty of her position was difficult. She describes the situation as "desert time," a time of wandering and wondering if they would even survive, let alone if they were going in the right direction. "Carol Ann and I tried to keep things going as best we could, always making sure that the things the Spirituality Network was known for — its hospitality and relationships — were maintained. We were always prayerful and determined to continue to offer people the opportunities to grow in their capacity to accept God's loving presence in their lives."

Through this "desert time," the seeds Noreen and the others had planted proved to be deep-rooted, however, with new shoots springing out and continuing to grow even in the arid conditions. "The Spirit was always with us," Amanda says. "Out of the conflict and chaos, there was new birth in the form of new people and new energy."

Barb expressed her feelings about the challenges and sense of renewed hope the Network experienced. "The past twelve months have been a time of challenge and discernment for the Network. Happily, at the end of this searching — and through God's help — we find ourselves ready to set out on another leg of the journey with renewed hope and vigor."

Barb noted that when Marianne Reihl retired after four stellar years of service, the Network received the gift of a new volunteer bookkeeper, Reva Allen. A new volunteer newsletter editor, Sandra Kerka, stepped up to take over another of Marianne's many roles. Barb said, "What became most apparent were the many amazing ways that God continues to provide for us as an organization."

Volunteers filling these two positions left funding for a new executive director. Patricia (Pat) Gibboney, a woman with a long list of accomplishments in nonprofit development, joined the staff in May of 2005. Barb describes Pat as exuding enthusiasm for the mission of the Network. "With her creative approach and many community alliances, we look forward to very special celebrations throughout the coming year."

Prior to joining the Network staff on a part-time basis, Pat had been working full-time as administrator at Rosemont Center in Columbus with the Sisters of the Good Shepherd. When the Network approached her about the role of executive director, she was told there were some challenges. Pat quickly responded, "With challenges there are opportunities."

Barb was excited to have Pat as the executive director. "There is an air of hopefulness and gratitude as we welcome Pat to our team. Pat brings a wealth of creative ideas and extensive experience in development and not-for-profit organizations. She adds great energy to our staff. Amanda Stone Cushing, our program coordinator, and Carol Ann Spencer, director of the Wellstreams program, will be working closely with Pat to increase excitement about the Network's presence and mission in the community."

Shortly after taking the executive director role at the Network, Pat had board members conduct a self-inventory to give her information about length of service, their expectations for the Network, as well as their expectations of her. In her work with the board, Pat asked them to try to come up with three names of individuals or organizations that could be introduced to the Network. Pat also asked the board members for their help to get the Network on more fiscally sound footing.

Pat took advantage of her relationships in Columbus to involve more people and to spread the Network's message. "Today we are experiencing a very exciting time as we celebrate our twentieth anniversary for the Network and the tenth anniversary for Wellstreams," she said. "It will be a time to reflect on the successes of the past and to look forward to the promises of the future. The Spirituality Network is now positioned to continue its work as an inclusive resource for individuals and groups who share a desire for spiritual growth."

Pat's enthusiasm was apparent from the beginning, and she proved to be a person with well thought out objectives as well and the plans to execute them. "We're strategizing. I think we are in the process right now of rebuilding relationships and building new relationships, and that takes time. One of the things I was concerned about was the people who had been involved many years ago who were no longer involved. The question to me was 'why?' I think the answer is probably a legitimate answer. Peoples' lives change, and it seems as though a lot of people come to the Network seeking spirituality because of a crisis or a life-changing event. We're trying to not only reach out to those people, but to people who aren't in that mode but really just want to go on the journey. It's a matter of trying to do outreach to as many congregations as possible. One of the things we need to find out is how to work more closely with clergy. Who are the decision makers? We want to let people know that we are a resource. I'm very excited."

As the Network's twentieth anniversary approached, the discernment process was complete. There was new enthusiasm and new hope for the future. But most important, the organization had reaffirmed its commitment to the thirsty traveler. With new resources, the ripples would continue to provide the cool, healing waters of spirituality so necessary for the journey to the God of love and forgiveness.

It felt good to know that the Spirituality Network had found another talented, resourceful and committed woman to lead them. Pat's remarks had impressed me, and I looked forward to meeting her just as I hoped to meet Noreen and Chris some day. I think what made me feel so good after reading the last chapter is that the Spirituality Network had once again walked that tightrope between dream and reality and had not fallen in the abyss. I'm not sure how many times they'd had to do that in their existence, but I couldn't help but see God's guiding hand in the result. I really felt good about where they were now. They had been proving themselves for twenty years, and I hoped they'd last another twenty … or more. I had one chapter left to read, and I started right in on it. I wanted to get this book back to Jean, thinking someone else might be waiting to read it. I would see Jean in another day when I met for spiritual direction.

ACROSS THE RIPPLES

To leave one's place of comfort is often difficult. It's much easier to cling to the warmth of the familiar, that which is not challenging. But for those who have heard the call of journey — an invitation to draw closer to the flame of God's love — the experience has often been life changing. The Spirituality Network has helped point out the path and then been that place of respite on the journey, a place where companions are available to help guide the way. Those who have been part of the Spirituality Network's journey over the past twenty years look back on its impact.

Frances Gabriel Mahoney: "My first memory of the Spirituality Network goes back to the general chapter. I remember turning and seeing Noreen standing. You know it takes great courage to stand up at a chapter and say your piece. Her expression to us was of this idea she had of some kind of body that would encourage others in their spiritual lives. And that we would do it. I thought she meant then as a community or congregation. And she did get the affirmation of the congregation. That is what I remember first."

Ron Atwood: "Is there somewhere I can go for a retreat? Is there someone in town who could lead our prayer group in a weekend of prayer? Are there any programs around to help support the unique spiritual needs of persons affected by AIDS? These were some of the questions that brought twenty-five people together twenty years ago. Our first response was compiling a list of resources, including capable persons and available facilities. This was the first networking. This listing generated many planning sessions. These sessions brought together creative persons who were committed to responding to the growing hunger for environments and opportunities in which individual persons could pray and reflect with others. Many, who had never before felt qualified to seek or help shape opportunities for spiritual enrichment, began to articulate their needs and offer their gifts. This was the second networking. From these early dreams and collaborations, the Spirituality Network has grown into an organized collective of people of different faith traditions, spiritual gifts, and life-circumstances committed to sharing the well of the Spirit."

Kerry Reed: "I was introduced to the Spirituality Network shortly after moving to Columbus in 1989. From my first attendance at an evening of worship and dance led by Otto Zing, I have valued the ecumenical and collegial attitude of the Network. Denominational ties of participants have paled by comparison to their desire to draw closer to the living God. The opportunity to be part of formalization of a training program for spiritual directors was a fulfillment of a yearning of my heart. When I get tired of the "endless" efforts to redefine the Network, I recall that we are in a constant state of becoming more of what the Spirit of God would have us be. Thank God for the Spirituality Network!"

Jeanne Purcell: "Once a week we'd have that special prayer day. It was so much a part of who we were. On the special prayer day, we would rotate the lead of it, and each person would introduce their own spirituality. I have to tell you each one of those times was like an epiphany for me. Time after time and day after day, step by step, led me to more healing. When I first came to the Network, I couldn't even receive the love; I was very limited. Step by step, inch by inch, that love penetrated the barrier. I am really a child of the Network. One of the big lessons of the

Network was the teaching of patience. Just waiting for God to do things on God's terms and in God's time. God has blessed me to be here to say this. There is nothing else I could cite besides the unconditional love that was expressed at the hands of these women to me."

Carol Ann Spencer: "It has been a wonderful and broadening experience to work in an ecumenical setting around the areas of spirituality and spiritual direction. Hungering for God knows no boundaries, and the journey always invites us into the more of the Mystery."

Corrine Hughes: "Being in the presence of people who are energized by the spiritual is powerful. And participating in the Network's unique spiritual programs has given me a greater awareness of God's Presence in both my private and public life. Divine Providence brought me to the Spirituality Network. I will be forever grateful."

Ellen Fox: "Simone Weil has wisely said, 'The danger is not lest the soul should doubt whether there is any bread, but lest, by a lie it should persuade itself that it is not hungry.' For me, the Network has always been about hunger. When I started direction with Noreen, she saw my hunger for

God and helped me find that space within myself. She then challenged me to live from that place. That led me to find my vocation as a massage therapist. When she blessed my hands it was a sacrament. I was called to go forth to bless and heal. That sense deepened as I went through the Wellstreams program and became a spiritual director. I also hungered for a community that would support me on my journey. The Network is a banquet of individuals who have enriched my life. It has given me a safe place to be fed and to feel the depth of my hunger. I am grateful."

Barb Davis: "Starting from Dominican roots, the Network is now a deeply ecumenical organization providing a variety of programs. Our mission is to foster spiritual growth. Many times recently I've heard people say things like 'I'm glad to find something like the Network. For the longest time I didn't know where to turn with my spiritual questions and desires.'"

Amanda Stone Cushing: "We are a surprise to many people — a very pleasant surprise. When they find us, they are amazed at what a resource we are to help them have a more personal relationship with God."

Marilyn Larkin: "I know that it is my interaction with the individuals I have met both at the Network and in the places that the association has led me, that has been my greatest blessing. Recognizing the God in them has brought me closer to God in me."

Dick Wood: "The original group was small, and for a long time it appeared that Sister Noreen, Sister Maxine and I, along with Father Vinny, would be 'the network,' but our prayers were answered and we grew and prospered. A look at the Spirituality Network today would support that conclusion. The organization has outstanding, committed leadership, and it seems evident that our best days are yet to come."

Sharon Reed: "In the past twenty years, I have realized the significance of the adage that 'the only constant is change.' However, in these same twenty years, I realize that the Spirituality Network has been one of the few constants in my life, even with all the change that has occurred in the Network itself. Even more, the guides and seekers and companions I have encountered through the relationships fostered by the Network have always assured me that God's abiding, merciful Presence is a constant that I can rely on and trust throughout all the changes and transformations that occur. I am so blessed to have been a part of all that *is* the Spirituality Network and to have witnessed the movement of the Spirit in myself, others, and the organization itself. I am called to pay attention to and honor these movements over the next twenty years and beyond – and to trust that God will continue to speak to me and others in wondrous ways, both joyful and painful. I will be ever grateful for those Dominican pioneers who first recognized my gifts and encouraged me to keep thirsting for God and even more grateful for the continuing companions who accompany me on the spiritual journey. I can only say, 'For all that has been – thanks! For all that will be – Yes!' (Hammarskjöld)"

Pat Gibboney: "What I think is certainly evident in my short time is that people that are touched by the Network are certainly transformed. The Network continues to be welcoming and non-judgmental for people who come through. I think sometimes we have to stop and realize that people are apprehensive about wanting to go on that journey. And how do we walk with them? I think that is critical. It sounds as if the mission is continuing the way it was. There have been a few bumps along the road, but it seems the mission is still to help people continue their journey."

But for every bump along the road, there has been a ripple in the gentle waters of the pond, a small wave of love and support from the center of this marvelous organization we call the Spirituality Network. Radiating from its center, the ripple moves out farther and farther, no longer aware of its surroundings, knowing only that it is on a journey, that wondrous trip we take to the center of the fire of God's love.

This time when I parked my car on the other side of the little park in front of Jean's house, I didn't make the trek with trepidation as I had just a few short weeks before. In fact, I was energized, thoroughly enjoying my walk. A lot had happened to me, and much of it was due to the binder I carried in my hand. Reading about the history of the Spirituality Network had provided me the hope and determination to pursue my own journey to the love and acceptance of an open-armed Creator. With the return of the book, I would be spending time with Jean as she guided me through my first session of spiritual direction.

I thought about the last chapter in the book on my short walk. It reminded me of the Parable of the Well that I had read in the opening of the book. Here were all these people from different faith experiences who had dipped their buckets deeply into the same well. The water of the Spirituality Network refreshed each of them, and, strengthened, they were able to continue on their journey. Their comments about that experience touched me deeply.

Jean greeted me warmly with a hug. When she took the binder from me, I noticed she handled it the same way she had when she'd given it to me, reverently, as if it were a holy book. She treated me with the same reverence during our session of spiritual direction, and I knew I would always be safe in her hands.

The cap to my experience, though, came as I made my way across the park to my car. Once again, I found myself gravitating to the forms on the basketball court. As I got closer, I could tell that the man and small boy I'd recognized before were together again on the court. This time, though, standing at the closed gate were two young girls, watching the play on the court with yearning eyes. "You girls want to play, too?" I asked.

"Yes," they said in unison.

"We can't get in, though," one of them added.

I reached up and unlatched the gate and pushed it open. The girls stood and looked at me. "It's OK," I said. "They'll let you play."

The two streamed through the gate and never looked back. I watched confidently as they approached the man and boy. I couldn't hear what was said, but it didn't take long for the two girls to be accepted into the game. The boy, who seemed to have learned so much about basketball since I'd first seen him, was demonstrating how to dribble while the man looked on. I caught his eye as I left, and he gave me a smile. I decided I'd leave the gate to the court open. Others might want to play as well. I began to hurry my walk. I was anxious to get home now. Jean had given me a brochure about a men's retreat that the Spirituality Network was holding in a couple of weeks, and I was anxious to talk to my husband about it. When you find good things, you need to share them. Right?

THE JOURNEY DOES NOT END

I thought the journey began only two-and-a-half
    years ago
    in the living room of the Lake House.
But it began so far, so long, I cannot remember
    when I was not on it. Did it begin
in the hair salon, where I read an article on
    direction?
    Did it begin when I first sang, "Praise God
from Whom all blessings flow" when I was
    eighteen months old?
    I have come to see, in the year of sitting
and being with another, companioning another,
    that the journey
    began many prayers, tears, desires ago.
I believed I would be a teacher, a guide, but
    instead I became
    a learner, a seeker, a fellow-traveler,
not only in their journeys, but in the journey
    inside myself. I am
    so much more than I believed, imagined;
less than my ego wanted me to be. Along the way
    are the gifts,
    the seeds and blossoms, wells and streams,
chrysalis, butterflies, all testifying that the
    journey has no end;
    the journey IS the end. The stories told to me
must touch the mystery of my own story. What still
    gives pain?
    Where must I too ask for healing, for mercy.
    We too
are seed, flower, chrysalis, butterfly. We too are
    the well.
    We too are the stream.

We make our journey, my companion and I,
    willing to blossom,
        to flow, to fly, to take in the wind of the Spirit,
    ever whispering on the way.
                        - Holly Bardoe

*The Joy of Sharing. Sharon Reed,
Ralph Huntzinger, Colleen Gallagher,
Carol Ann Spencer*

AFTERWORD

In Autumn 2003, Noreen Malone celebrated fifty years as a Dominican sister. Reflecting on her years of thirsting for the Divine and how her thirst led to the Network, she wrote, "As I begin a week's retreat preparing to celebrate, I am deeply aware of how very thirsty I still am. This thirst has been with me for as long as I can remember, even before I entered St. Mary of the Springs in 1951. These fifty years have filled me with a passion for encouraging people to experience the God who loves them unconditionally. What a jubilee blessing it would be for me if everyone who reads this would see their own story in this reflection rather than mine. I pray you will take some time to ponder how God has been present in your life — in each moment, circumstance, blessing, suffering, person or transition — always at work quenching your thirst. Together we can give thanks to a Faithful God!"

A Women-to-Women Gathering

ABOUT THE AUTHORS

WAYNE RAPP, a member of the Spirituality Network board, is a graduate of the University of Arizona with a major in English. He currently lives in Columbus, Ohio, and works as a freelance writer. His company, It's a Rapp Productions, also produces films and videos for agencies and corporate clients. His nonfiction has appeared in a variety of publications, including *The Columbus Dispatch* and *AirFare.* A book written for the Ohio Arts Council, *Celebrating, Honoring, and Valuing Rich Traditions: The History of the Ohio Appalachian Arts Program,* was published in 2006. His essay, "Lessons From Underground," is part of the Bottom Dog Press collection *Writing Work: Writers on Working Class Writing.* Another essay, "Exporting America," was published in the 2007 edition of *Out of Line: Writings on Issues of Peace and Justice.* His video, "Life — The First Gift," produced for the Heinzerling Foundation, is the Winner of the Bronze Quill Award from the International Association of Business Communicators. Wayne's fiction has appeared in High Plains Literary Review, Vincent Brothers Review, Grit, Thema, Chiricú, The Americas Review, Mississippi Review, the Bottom Dog Press Anthology, *Working Hard for the Money,* the Fall Creek Press series, *VeriTales,* and in the Bilingual Press Anthology, *Latinos in Lotusland.* Wayne's fiction has twice been honored with fellowships from the Ohio Arts Council. His short story "In the Time of Marvel and Confusion," was nominated for inclusion in the Pushcart Prize Series. A recently completed collection of border stories, *Burnt Sienna,* was a finalist for the 2005 Miguel Mármol Prize for Fiction. Wayne, the father of four and grandfather of eight, is a member of St. Thomas the Apostle Catholic Church.

RICK HATEM, a spiritual director, has received spiritual direction himself for twenty years. A former member of the Spirituality Network board, he has also represented that organization on the board of the Columbus Metropolitan Area Church Council. Rick formerly was employed in communications for the Catholic Diocese of Columbus. In 1986, after completing work for a master's degree in journalism from Ohio State, he moved to Jerusalem where he volunteered in a hospitality house that tried to create dialogue with Israelis and Palestinians. While performing the volunteer work, he was introduced to *l'Arche,* an international community started by Jean Vanier for adults and children with developmental disabilities and those who live with them and assist them. For much of the next fifteen years, Rick lived in l'Arche communities on three continents. For three of those years, he led a community in Stratford, Ontario, Canada. L'Arche subscribes to mutuality, the belief that all were created to be creative, that each of us has something to offer to others even when it is not immediately apparent. His experiences in l'Arche led to his involvement in spiritual direction. Rick returned to Ohio in 2001 to assist his parents with the increasing challenges of independent living while aging (his mother was diagnosed with Alzheimer's disease about seven years ago). His parents live in Vinton County, where Rick is a member of St. Sylvester Catholic Church in Zaleski, Ohio.

ANNE RAPP has been associated with the Spirituality Network from its earliest days. She has been in spiritual direction for over ten years. Anne, a graduate of the State University of New York in Oswego, is a teacher with experience in three states: New York, California, and Ohio. She was voted "Outstanding New Teacher" in the Norwalk-La Mirada (CA) School District in her first year. Besides her work as a teacher in Columbus, Ohio, she was active in her parish, St. Philip the Apostle, working on a number of projects and committees. Adult Education was of particular interest to her, and she organized and produced a number of adult education programs. After leaving education, Anne turned her background in English and her writing talents to editing. She was employed by Rockwell International and the Secretary of State's office in that capacity. She later began working on her own as a freelance editor, providing services for public relations and marketing companies, advertising agencies and corporations such at the AT&T Training Center and Macmillan/McGraw-Hill. She is a member of Writers' Bloc, an organization affiliated with the Thurber House. She is also a member of several prayer groups and is one of the founders of the Women's Respite Program in Columbus and currently serves as vice president of its board. Anne plays an active supporting role in the lives of her children and grandchildren and worships at St. Thomas the Apostle Church.

Rick Hatem took on the Herculean effort of researcher, recording the recollections of all those who responded to the Network's invitation to help tell the story. He recorded nine and a half hours of memories, then spent more than forty hours on the arduous task of transcribing and organizing information. Rick spent another two hundred fifty hours reading, selecting, and editing material from newsletters and other records at the Network office. Before he had completed his task, he'd spent around five hundred hours scattered over fifteen months.

Wayne Rapp took the 269 pages of transcriptions (some of it single spaced) and began to cut and paste as he reorganized and found the threads that he could weave into a narrative flow.

Anne Rapp either selected or wrote the meditations that separate the chapters yet tie them together as a complete story. She also edited the entire manuscript to assure a more readable experience.

In true Spirituality Network fashion, this was a collaborative effort: the combining of skills to articulate this ongoing endeavor. We writers strived to be faithful to the inspiration that helped create and sustain the Spirituality Network for twenty years. We contributed our talents as best we could, realizing that with all of our effort, we did not tell a complete story. For those we may have slighted in our effort, we apologize. It was not intentional, only human frailty at work. It is our hope that this account of the dream at work in us has awakened the dream in the reader, so that the stone of awareness in each person may continue to send ripples of peace and justice into the wanting world.

ATTRIBUTIONS

Maxine Shonk, OP, "Parable of the Well." Reprinted by permission of the author.

Edwina Gateley, "The Sharing" and "Stirrings" from *Psalms of a Laywoman,* © 1999 by Edwina Gateley. Reprinted by permission of Sheed & Ward, an imprint of Rowman & Littlefield Publishing, Inc. http:www.rowmanlittlefield.com/Sheed/

Liz Kaercher, the photograph "Rippling Water." Reprinted by permission of the photographer.

Mary Oliver, "Wild Geese" and "The Journey" from *Dream Work,* © 1986 by Mary Oliver. Reprinted by permission of The Atlantic Monthly Press.

Holly Bardoe, "Shedding the Chrysalis" and "The Journey Does Not End." Reprinted by permission of the author.

Daniel E. Schleppi, the photograph and reflection "Guide and Traveler." Reprinted by permission of the photographer and writer.

Ron Atwood, the reflection "Woman at the Well," written for the *Lenten Journal,* February 27, 2005. Reprinted by permission of the author.

Sandra Kerka, Arti Gras photographs. Reprinted by permission of the photographer.

MORE INFORMATION ABOUT THE SPIRITUALITY NETWORK

The Spirituality Network is an ecumenical organization, serving seekers of the living water both within and outside of religious institutions. Among the resources it provides travelers on their spiritual journeys are:

- Education and formation through the Wellstreams training program
- Spiritual direction referrals for groups and individuals
- Retreat planning and facilitation
- Programs to foster the spiritual life
- Connection to a variety of other spirituality resources in central Ohio
- Women-to-Women Listening Circles

For more information on programs and resources, contact the Spirituality Network at:

444 East Broad Street
Columbus, OH 43215
Office: (614) 228-8867
Fax: (614) 228-8975
spiritnetwk@hotmail.com

www.spiritualitynetwork.org/

Wellstreams

Wellstreams is an ecumenical program of spiritual formation and training in the art of spiritual direction. The Wellstreams program honors in each individual this ever-deepening cycle of awareness and empowerment. It is a two-phase program designed to enhance the personal spiritual growth of participants and provide training in spiritual direction and companioning. Phase One begins with an opening weekend retreat. Classes are held on two Wednesday evenings and two Saturday mornings per month during the first year, ending with a group retreat to discern readiness for the next phase. Phase Two classes meet four Wednesday evenings per month with several Saturday workshops each semester. Participants are expected to be in spiritual direction throughout the duration of the program.

To discover more about Wellstreams, e-mail carol.spencer1@juno.com or call 614-228-8867. The Wellstreams web site is located at the following address: www.spiritualitynetwork.org/wellstreamsprogram.html